The Shattered Lantern

Also by Ronald Rolheiser

Against an Infinite Horizon
Forgotten Among the Lilies
The Restless Heart
Seeking Spirituality

The Shattered Lantern

Rediscovering God's presence
in everyday life

Ronald Rolheiser

Hodder & Stoughton
LONDON SYDNEY AUCKLAND

Permission to quote the poems on pp. 138 and 161 is
gratefully acknowledged.

10 9 8 7 6 5 4 3 2 1

ISBN 0 340 61253 3

Typeset by Phoenix Typesetting, Ilkley, West Yorkshire.

Printed and bound in Great Britain by
The Guernsey Press Co. Ltd, Guernsey, C.I.

Hodder and Stoughton Ltd
A division of Hodder Headline PLC
338 Euston Road
London NW1 3BH

I dedicate the book to my mother and father, Mathilda and George, who taught me never to ridicule anyone who is searching for God with a lighted lantern.

Contents

Contents

Acknowledgements

Many persons, more than I can name, helped me in the writing of this book. Some, however, should be named:

I thank first of all my community, the Oblates of Mary Immaculate of St Mary's Province, Canada, who, despite my many shortcomings, never waver in how much they trust me and how much they entrust to me. The same is true of my family, that large clan of sisters and brothers and nieces and nephews, whose patience with me knows no bounds. A very special thanks to Tony Dummer omi and the Oblates at Old St Mary's Church, Oakland, California, who provided me with the kind of hospitality that makes for a good space within which to write a book – good fellowship, a well-laden table, a daily Eucharist, and a beautiful old room with a hardwood floor and a bay window.

Finally, a huge thanks to Eric Major and everyone at Hodder and Stoughton for adopting this exile, especially to Carolyn Armitage, my editor, for her gentle persistence in reminding me of approaching deadlines, her gracious forgiveness in handling missed deadlines, and her tact and professional eye in suggesting revisions.

Nietzsche's madman and the smashed lantern

In real life you get a history; in folklore you get a story. In the real world you get time; in folklore you get once upon a time. So, with a little help from Nietzsche, a story...

Once upon a time – in a time quite other than our own, but in a time that might have been our own – there was a town which was like every other town. It had, at its centre, a market-square where the people came to meet each other and to do business. One day at noon, when the sun was high and all was busyness and business, a madman rushed into that market-square carrying a lighted lantern and shouting: 'I seek God! I seek God!' The people were both irritated and amused: 'Has God got lost? Is he hiding? Is he like a little child that loses his way?' they asked. But the madman went to the centre of the square, smashed his lantern on the pavement, and shouted: 'You won't find God! God is dead and we are his murderers! And how did we do this? With what kind of sponge can we wipe away a whole horizon?'

Nietzsche's madman and the smashed lantern

Part I

Narcissism, pragmatism, unbridled restlessness, and the loss of the ancient instinct for astonishment

'The greatest of all illusions is the illusion of familiarity.'
(G. K. Chesterton)

Chapter 1

The problem of unbelief among believers

THE AGNOSTICISM OF OUR ORDINARY CONSCIOUSNESS

One of the most famous novels of all time begins with the words: 'All happy families resemble each other, each unhappy family is unhappy in its own way.'[1]

What is true of families, is also true of generations, each is unique in its unhappiness. Our own is no exception, particularly in its religious struggles. Where past generations of believers unhappily fought over questions of church, the correct interpretation of scripture, and the uniqueness and place of Christ, our own religious struggle focuses on the most central of all questions, the existence of God.

We live in an age of unbelief. What sets this apart from past generations is that, today, this is often as true within religious circles as outside them. The problem of faith today is especially that of unbelief among believers.

Belief in God, for many of us, is little more than a hangover. We feel the effects of a religious activity of the past, but our own consciousness borders on agnosticism. Rarely is there a vital sense of God within the bread and butter of life. We still make a certain space for God within our churches, but God is given a very restricted place everywhere else.

A hundred years ago when Friedrich Nietzsche made his famous declaration that God is dead, he was not so much suggesting that God had died in the heavens as he was saying that God no longer really mattered in day-to-day life, save as a

15

hangover. God is dead, but his 'shadow is a long one, and we must first conquer this shadow.'[2]

Contemporary analyst, Philip Rieff, says much the same thing. In his view, our generation has an ambivalent relationship towards God: God has disappeared but we still have his calling card. He is absent but, because of our religious past, we still have a connection. Future generations, he asserts, will not even have his calling card.[3]

These images, faith as a hangover, religion as struggling with God's shadow, and an absent God whose calling card we still possess, describe, at least in terms of a wide generalisation, our everyday struggle with faith and agnosticism. We still have some experience of God, though rarely is this a vital one wherein we actually drink, first-hand, from living waters. Most often, in so far as God does enter our everyday experience, God is not experienced as a living person to whom we actually talk, person to person, from whom we seek final consolation and comfort, and to whom we relate friend to friend, lover to lover, child to parent.

Rather God is experienced and related to as a religion, a church, a moral philosophy, a guide for private virtue, an imperative for justice, or as a nostalgia for proper propriety. For most of us, belief in God resembles the following: God is religion and religion represents a way of life – churchgoing; guidance from the Bible; sex within monogamous marriage; no lying, cheating, or swearing; democratic principles; proper aesthetics; and being nice to each other.

For most of us, then, God is more of a moral and intellectual principle than a person and our commitment to this principle runs the gamut from fiery passion, wherein persons are willing to die for a cause, to a vague nostalgia, wherein God and religion are given the same type of status and importance as is given the royal family in England, namely, they are the symbolic anchor for a certain way of life but they are hardly important in its day-to-day functioning. It is not that this is bad, it is just that one does not see much evidence that anyone is actually all that interested in God. We are interested in virtue, justice, a proper way of life, and perhaps even in building communities for worship, support, and justice, but, in the end, too much evidence suggests that moral philosophies, human instinct, and

16

a not so disguised self-interest are more important in motivating these activities than are a love and a gratitude that stem from a personal relationship to a living God. Hence, God is not only often absent in our marketplaces, he is also frequently absent from our religious activities (and religious fervour) as well.

This suggests, as mentioned earlier, that there is more than a little unbelief among us believers. God is a hangover, a neurosis, a calling card, a religion, a cause ... and only rarely a living, informing, comforting, challenging person whose reality dwarfs that of our everyday world.

In his book, *The Gay Science*, Nietzsche presents this scenario: A madman lights a lantern and, in bright daylight, rushes into a crowded marketplace shouting: 'I seek God! I seek God!'[4] But the people in the marketplace ridicule him: 'Has he got lost?' asks one. 'Did he lose his way like a child?' asks another. 'Is he hiding? Or is he afraid of us?' The people yell and laugh at him. Then the madman turns on them and shouts: 'God is dead, I tell you, we have killed him, you and I. All of us are his murderers. But how did we do this? How could we drink up the sea? Who gave us the sponge to wipe away the entire horizon? What was the holiest and mightiest of all that the world has yet owned has bled to death under our knives.' Then he, the madman, goes silent, smashes his lantern on the ground, and announces: 'I have come too early. This deed is still too distant for people to see, and yet they have done this to themselves. They have killed God!'

How can someone kill God? What Nietzsche is suggesting with this parable is that unbelief, a certain kind of atheism, is not something which exists primarily outside the circle of those people who take themselves as believers. It is, first of all, a phenomenon within the circle of believers. Simply put, the problem of atheism and unbelief is not so much that the existence of God is denied by certain persons, but that God is absent from the ordinary consciousness and lives of believers, God is not enough alive or important in ordinary consciousness. It is in this way, in the words of Nietzsche's madman, 'that we have killed him.'

Why is this? Why is God not more alive within our ordinary lives and consciousness? Two possible explanations exist; both have their conscientious presenters and both can function simultaneously since they are not, in the end, mutually exclusive.

17

John of the Cross once wrote that a silence of God can occur within experience because God can be 'obscure' or because we can be 'blind' ... an object can be vague because it is too distant or because we have bad eyesight.[5] Hence, God can positively withdraw his presence in order to purify our faith ('obscurity'), or we can have a weak experience of God because there is something wrong with us ('blindness'). The former he calls 'a dark night of the soul', the latter he calls a fault in contemplation.

Recent theological debate has, in fact, polarised a lot around this very distinction. Conservatives and liberals both agree that our experience of God today is far from what it might be. After this they differ. Conservatives, by and large, attribute the problem to what John of the Cross would term 'blindness', there is something wrong with the way we are living and this makes the experience of God difficult. Liberals, on the other hand, tend to understand the issue more in line with John's term 'obscurity', our experience of God is weak because we are being purified and led through a dark night of the soul to a more mature experience of God. Who is right?

Obviously this needs careful discernment. Moreover, these interpretations are not mutually exclusive. Always, in every age, we will struggle with faith both because God positively tests us by withdrawing a certain consoling presence and because we are never as faithful as we should be. God is always partially obscure and we are always partially blind.

It is not my purpose here to comment on the debate as to whether our present experience of God is weak because God is leading us to a deeper level of faith or because there is something not fully right with us. It is always a bit of both. This book, however, wants to focus on the latter, that which is wrong with us. I choose this route not because I feel that the conservative thesis is more valid than the liberal one, but because we cannot, in the end, do anything about God's freedom, about whether or not God chooses to give us dark nights of the soul. We can however do something about our disposition towards God. Hence our focus will be on our struggles in faith in so far as these constitute a certain fault on our part.

What is less than perfect within us that dulls and muddies our experience of God? If each age is unique in its unhappiness, what is at the root of our own unhappy religious struggle?

When dealing with the struggle to experience God, the issue obviously is not so much one of God's presence or absence as it is one of the presence or absence of God *within our awareness*. God is always present, but we are not always present to God. As one spiritual writer puts it, 'God is no more present in a church than in a drinking bar, but, generally, we are more present to God in a church than in a bar.'[6]

Jesus says, 'blessed are the pure of heart for they shall see God.'[7] Awareness of God is, for him, attached to a certain state of mind and heart, namely, purity of heart. Classical spiritual writers have always identified purity of heart with contemplation. Hence the struggle to purify consciousness so as to better experience God is the struggle for contemplation, for a fuller awareness. In Western culture today – and this, in caption, is the thesis of this book – most of us have an atrophied contemplative faculty, a muddied self-awareness. God is present to us, but we are not present to God. We lack contemplativeness and because of this we lack a vital experience of God. The eclipse of God in ordinary awareness is, in the end, a fault in contemplation. What does this mean?

THE ECLIPSE OF GOD AS A FAULT IN CONTEMPLATION

How is our self-awareness muddied? How, precisely, do we lack purity of heart?

Experience has shades of quality, degrees of openness. We are aware and awake according to more or less. Given this, God can be very present within an event but we can be so self-preoccupied and focused upon our headaches, heartaches, tasks, daydreams, and restless distractions that we can be oblivious to that presence.

Heartaches, headaches, pressing tasks, distracting restlessness – *narcissism, pragmatism*, and *unbridled restlessness*, as we shall later name these – severely limit what we are aware of within ordinary experience. Normally there is a huge gap between what we are actually aware of and what is radically available for us to be aware of within experience. Thus, awareness or non-awareness of God within ordinary experience depends upon the quality and depth of our ordinary experience in general. We can be asleep or awake to where God appears. That quality of awareness, or lack of it, in ordinary life is what contemplation is all about.

Contemplation is about waking up. Simply defined, to be contemplative is to experience an event fully, in all its aspects. Biblically this is expressed as knowing 'face to face'.[8] What is implied in that phrase – and the task of this whole book will be to explicate it – is that we are in contemplation when we stand before reality and experience it without the limits and distortions that are created by narcissism, pragmatism, and excessive restlessness.

To be contemplative is to be fully awake to all the dimensions within ordinary experience. And, classical spiritual writers assure us, if we are awake to all that is there within ordinary experience, if our ordinary awareness is not reduced or distorted through excessive narcissism, pragmatism, or restlessness, there will be present in it, alongside everything else that makes up experience, a sense of the infinite, the sacred, God. That, in brief, is the thesis of this book. When we are fully awake to ordinary experience, it brings with it a certain *contuition* of God.[9] Conversely, when our ordinary awareness is reduced or distorted, when it is not contemplative, God dies in our awareness and eventually in our churches as well.

Hence our struggle with unbelief, the struggle to make God more real in ordinary life, is really a struggle with contemplation. But are we not natural contemplatives? Have not developments within psychology and the social sciences given us deeper self-understanding? Do we not, today, more than ever before, crave solitude, peace and quiet?

We are natural contemplatives; psychology and the social sciences have significantly deepened our self-understanding, and we do crave solitude and quiet. However none of these necessarily mean that we are in fact, in our daily lives, contemplative. What is obvious is that our sense of God is weak. This can only mean that our contemplative sense is likewise weak. Why is this so, if so many factors seemingly indicate the opposite?

In answering this question one must resist the temptation to be either unduly negative or uncritical of our culture. We tend to be optimists or pessimists, liberals or conservatives, by temperament and, accordingly, it is easy to be overly critical or overly generous in assessing any situation. In critically assessing our culture it is necessary therefore, first of all, to point out its ambivalence. It has both strengths and weaknesses, with its weaknesses often being the shadow side of its strengths. However, with that necessary acknowledgement, it is, I submit, clear that interiority and contemplation are not its strengths. Theologian, Jan Walgrave, once commented that 'our age constitutes a virtual conspiracy against the interior life.'[10]

What is implied here? Obviously the reference is not to a deliberate conspiracy, deviously and consciously designed by some group with a vested interest in destroying values, but to an accidental confluence of historical circumstances, a conspiracy of accidents, now meeting in Western history which, simply put, are making it harder for us to live the examined life.

What are these forces that are conspiring against the interior life? A rather simplistic view, all too common today, submits that today's faith struggles have their roots in the social changes of the 1960s. Rock music, the Beatles, the Vietnam war, drugs, the sexual revolution, affluence and the emergence of the first real post rags-to-riches generation, new technologies, and new opportunities for travel and anonymity, it suggests, changed our conception of family, marriage, morality, and of God and religion. Life in the Western world changed rather fundamentally in the last three decades and, with that change, the old ideals of family and religion were undermined. Problems with faith today are then rooted in the social changes that have occurred within the last generation.

This is too simplistic. When Nietzsche's madman smashes his lantern and shouts: 'God is dead and we are his murderers!' the murdering process that he is referring to is one which has taken place gradually, almost imperceptibly, through many centuries. Any generation that feels that God is dead is at the end of a long historical process which killed God unknowingly, gradually, imperceptibly, and often with the very means it was employing in trying to keep him alive.[11]

The reason why our generation struggles with a certain practical atheism has its roots in changes that began in Western history centuries ago, with the birth of the Renaissance and the advent of modern science and modern philosophy. A seed was

21

planted then which has only come to full bloom in the latter part of this century. Hence the roots of our present crisis of belief have tentacles which reach back many centuries.

What are these roots? They are an extremely complex mixture of historical, philosophical, cultural, psychological, moral, and religious factors that began hundreds of years ago. This must be stated clearly and kept in mind, even though this book, whose purpose is modest, will not attempt to lay out those roots for close examination.[12] Instead the next two chapters analyse how, given what has grown from those roots in our culture it is becoming increasingly difficult for us not to be practical atheists, even as we still profess belief in God and go to our churches.

Notes

1) Leo Tolstoy, *Anna Karenina*, Pt i, chapt. I, Translation by Maude.

2) Friedrich Nietzsche, *The Gay Science*, ET. W. Kaufmann, NY, Vintage Books, 1974, p. 167.

3) Philip Rieff, *The Triumph of the Therapeutic*, NY, Harper Torchbooks, 1966.

4) This, and the subsequent quotations in this paragraph, are taken from F. Nietzsche, *The Gay Science*, Book 3, no. 125, the edition cited above, p. 182.

5) John of the Cross, *The Living Flame of Love*, Commentary on Stanza 3, numbers 70–76, translated by K. Kavanaugh and O. Rodriquez, ICS Publications, Washington, DC. 1979, pp. 637–640.

6) Sheila Cassidy, *Prayer for Pilgrims*, London, 1980, p. 61.

7) Matthew 5:8.

8) 1 Corinthians 13:12–13.

This definition of contemplation as coming 'face to face' with God, others, and the cosmos, is the way many of the classical writers in spirituality, precisely, define contemplation; e.g., John of the Cross.

9) This term, *contuition* (which will take on some importance in Chapter 6) needs some explanation as to its origins and meaning.

Regarding its origins: this is a term which was originally coined by a Benedictine monk of Stanbrook (who published under that name), *Medieval Mystical Tradition and John of the Cross*, London, 1954, p. 70. Austin Farrer uses it in his famous philosophical essay, *Finite and Infinite: A Philosophical Essay*, Westminster, 1943. Farrer says that *within ordinary perception*, if ordinary perception is fully open to all the dimensions of reality, one perceives ('contuits'), *alongside* the finite, the infinite.

Hence, as regards its meaning: it is not exactly synonymous with the term *intuition*. In intuitive knowing something is grasped beyond what is strictly warranted by perception and the logical reasoning processes that follow upon perception. In contuition you have insight which goes beyond strict sense perception, but, as we will see in detail in Chapter 6, this insight is had *alongside* and *as part of* ordinary sense perception and, consequently, is 'warranted' by ordinary perception. It is, as we will see, precisely the contemplative dimension of perception.

10) In private conversation. That conversation, however, is expanded into a short article. (See: Ronald Rolheiser, *Just too Busy to Bow Down*, in, *Forgotten Among the Lilies*, London, Hodder and Stoughton, 1990, pp. 12–114.

11) We often kill God by bad religion. Atheism is, most often, generated by bad theism. Michael Buckley, in a monumental (though difficult to read) book, *At the Origins of Modern Atheism*, (New Haven, Yale University Press, 1987) lays out the plumbing of this in a way that perhaps nobody, till now, has done.

12) For an analysis of those historical roots, see: Ronald Rolheiser, 'The Deeper Causes Underlying our Present Difficulties in Believing', to appear in *Louvain Studies*, 1994.

Chapter 2

Narcissism, pragmatism, unbridled restlessness and the non-contemplative personality

FACTORS MILITATING AGAINST CONTEMPLATION

Jesus promised that if we have purity of heart, we shall see God. What, exactly, blocks this purity of heart? If God is there to be experienced, why is God not more urgent within our experience? Why do we so often confuse the experience of God with our own projects and self-interests? Why is our normal awareness not more open and less muddied?

1) *Narcissism*
Prior to the birth of philosophy, ancient Greece crystallised much of its religious and psychological wisdom into a series of myths. One such myth is that of Narcissus.

Narcissus was the son of the river god, Cephissus, and a youth of surpassing beauty and vanity. A mountain nymph, Echo, fell in love with him, but he was cold to her. Eventually she pined away to a mere voice because her love for him found no response. Because of this, the god, Nemesis, determined to punish Narcissus for his vanity and so caused him to go for a drink at a certain pool of water in which he would see his reflection. Seeing his image, Narcissus was overcome with the sense of his own beauty to the point where he fell in love with himself and became obsessed with his own beauty. Thus, turned inward and paralysed by his obsession with himself, he eventually withered away and became a flower which still bears his name.

Freudian psychology has picked up this myth and now uses its name as a technical term within psychoanalysis. Simply defined, for them, narcissism means excessive self-preoccupation.

Few images are as apt to describe the contemporary mindset as is that of narcissism. If we are not a generation in love with itself, we are, undeniably, one that is obsessed with itself. There is an abundance of literature which analyses this in great detail and it is not necessary here to summarise it. It is sufficient for our purposes to offer just one example.

We see this narcissism, first of all, in our propensity for individualism and our corresponding inability to be healthily aware of and concerned about reality beyond our private lives. To offer a simple, but clear illustration: For the past some years, I have been involved in helping offer a marriage preparation course. This course is, for the people attending it, a requirement without which they cannot obtain permission to be married within their various churches. Hence many who are attending are not there because of their own wish. In our sessions, we do battle with their many objections. These objections rarely deal with the substance of what is being discussed, the nature of marriage. Rather, and this is what is revealing, the primary objection (often hostile) is always to the idea of the course itself: 'Why do we have to take this course? Why are the church and society concerned about *my* marriage? *My* marriage is nobody's business. This is *my* life, *my* love, *my* sex, *my* honeymoon, *my* future, *my* concern!'

These questions and objections, innocent enough in themselves, are revealing because they betray an individualism, a lack of the sense of the corporate, and a lack of a sense of reality outside private concern that is, in the end, seriously unhealthy. One hears objections like this more from the children of Rene Descartes than from the children of Jesus Christ. When the great philosopher, Rene Descartes, 1596–1650, was searching for an indubitable starting point for his philosophy, he doubted the reality of everything he could until he came to a reality that he could not doubt: '*I think, therefore, I am!*' In Descartes' mind, what we can be sure of, what we know is real, is ourselves. We might be dreaming everything else.

Listening to the objections of the young people that I just quoted, one hears, like an echo, the lonely voice of Descartes doubting the reality of everything beyond the private world of his own self: 'I think, therefore, I am ... my heartaches, my headaches, my wounds, my problems, my chronic shortage of money, my mortgage, my tasks, and my worries are real. Other people's lives and the larger community and its concerns are not as real.'

This type of self-centredness is not surprising, nor unique to our age. The very structure of the human personality, as a centre of self-awareness, makes us by nature narcissistic. Much of our childhood experience further enhances this. Our own reality is always the paramount one. To ourselves we are always massively real. Today however, as will be shown in the next chapter, a conspiracy of accidents has helped intensify our natural proclivity for self-preoccupation to the point where we are unhealthily obsessed with, and entrapped within, ourselves.

Narcissism, in so far as it adversely affects contemplation, is characterised, today, by four salient features:

i) The incapacity to recognise sufficiently the reality of others

This characteristic is very evident in the example just given. These young people with their objections ('This is *my* marriage, it is nobody else's business!') are the children of our culture, incarnations of its basic attitudes. In them, we see the struggle we all have to see others and the world outside us as being as real as we are.

ii) The yuppie instinct for the quality of life

Currently we are witnessing something which has been termed the *yuppie phenomenon*. The term may not sound serious, but the reality it describes is one of the more significant recent developments in Western culture.

What is a yuppie?[1]

We guide our lives more by unconscious myth and feeling than we do by rationality and so we may define the term yuppie by four interpenetrating slogans: Quality of Life, Upward Mobility, The Pursuit of Excellence, and Material Comfort.

The unconscious, and in many cases the conscious, mythology that moves people today is that of success, of moving up the ladder, of being rich, of having a beautiful body, of being well-dressed, of having prestige, of luxuriating in material comfort, of achieving optimally, but in comfort, everything that is potentially attainable with our limits. In many cases, this brings with it unashamed ambition and the expressed desire, in a manner of speaking, to leave the pack behind. An important part of the quality of being a yuppie is to set oneself, through excellence, above others.

Obviously, not all of this is bad, nor novel. People have always wanted these things and the myths of past generations (e.g., rags to riches, work hard and get ahead) hardly seem different. As well, there is nothing inherently immoral in these things, nor is the emphasis on excellence something that should be prophetically challenged. What is novel, less moral, and needs prophetic challenge in the yuppie attitude is that, here, pursuit of excellence and quality of life are tied to an explicit philosophy of life within which unbridled individualism, selfishness, and idiosyncratic development are unabashedly held up as virtues. Salvation is self-development, pure and simple. Everything – marriage, family, community, justice, church, morality, service to others, sacrifice – makes sense, takes its place, and has value only in so far as it enhances idiosyncratic development. In Greek, the word *Idios* means 'a movement towards one's own.' What the yuppie espouses and nurtures, both inside self and within society at large, is precisely the movement towards self. Self-development is pursued with a sense of duty and asceticism that were formerly reserved for religion because, for the yuppie, self-development is salvation, it is the religious project.

How deeply we are influenced by this ideal is evident in a variety of ways. Among other things, we see it by looking at what we read and by looking at what we admire.

When we survey the best-seller lists for non-fiction books in recent years, we see that virtually every one of these books has to do with achievement, the rewards of success, the quality of lifestyle, and the pursuit of excellence. We also see this in the proclivity we have for the rich and the famous. Neil Postman, in *Amusing Ourselves to Death*, describes the 1983 commencement exercises at Yale University. Several honorary doctorates were awarded, including one to Mother Theresa. As she and the others, each in turn, received their degrees, the audience applauded appropriately, but with, as Postman says, a slight hint of reserve and impatience, 'for it wished to give its heart to the final recipient who waited shyly in the wings.' As the details of her achievements were read, many of the audience left their seats and surged towards the stage. Finally, when the name of the final recipient was announced, Meryl Streep, the audience 'unleashed a sonic boom of affection, enough to wake the New Haven dead.'[2] This is not intended as a criticism of Meryl Streep. She is a fine actress and, by all indications, a fine human being as well. The point of recounting the incident is the audience's reaction. In their response, again one which is typical of our culture, we see what we value most highly.

Ultimately, this is narcissism, perhaps not as the textbooks lay it out, but certainly of the sort that Freud would recognise. We are a culture very much caught up in the idiosyncratic.

iii) The movement towards excessive privacy

One of the features of narcissism is the movement towards excessive privacy. Looking at our culture we see a relentless movement towards greater privatisation in virtually every area of life. For us, the ideal is to have a private car, a private office, a private home; and, then, within that home, to have a private room, a private bathroom, a private phone, a private stereo system, and a private television set and video recorder.

Perhaps nothing is more apt, as a single image, to depict the movement towards excessive privacy than is the image of a shopper in a busy supermarket who has radio headphones covering his or her ears. While overtly very public and potentially social, they are moving inside their own private world. Speak of the idiosyncratic, or receding into a private world!

The very ideal of law within most of Western culture also betrays this demand for excessive privacy. For most of us, the ideal of law and order is that of the *Pax Romanum*, namely, law should maintain enough public order so that everyone can do his or her own private thing. By most standards in the West, that is the definition of human rights.

Again, there is nothing inherently wrong with privacy. No one comes to maturity, or stays there, except through a healthy balance of social interaction and privacy. What is at issue is the excessive need for privacy. When this is unchecked then meaningful social interaction diminishes and the opportunity is there for us to escape into a world of private projects, private dreams, and private fantasies. Narcissism grows stronger when there is not enough meaningful social interaction to draw us out of our private selves and make us aware that reality outside us is just as real as we are. This movement towards greater privacy is both a symptom and a cause of narcissism.

iv) The inability to act out of a purpose beyond the idiosyncratic preference

In Western culture today, more and more, we are so preoccupied with our own inner worlds that we find it difficult to act out of any motivation beyond that of doing our own thing.

Sociologist, Robert Bellah, gives an excellent example of this. He begins his fine book, *Habits of the Heart*,[3] with the story of Brian, a young Californian businessman. Brian is a man who has, in his own mind, changed his value system after the trauma of a divorce. As a youth, he had given himself over to the pursuit of pleasure: 'hell-raising and sex'. Later he married, settled down, assumed a very responsible job, and fathered three children. His marriage, while not an unhappy one for him, was not the focus of his life. His work and career were. He worked 65–70 hours a week and seldom took weekends off. His career skyrocketed, his marriage died. One night he came home to an empty house. His wife had left him.

The divorce was a major shock. Unaccustomed to failure of any kind, the demise of his marriage provoked in him a crisis which eventually led him to radically alter his priorities. When he finally remarried, marriage and family life became something different for him. Formerly, he had sacrificed everything for his job, his career, and his company. Now what was primary in his life was his family. When something had to be sacrificed it now was the job that got shortchanged. Brian is now happy and has a new sense of energy and enthusiasm which he attributes to his family and his new sense of priorities. Family life is now the centre from which he draws energy and meaning.

In many ways, this sounds like a conversion story. The difficulty arises, as Bellah points out, when Brian tries to explain why his present life is better than his former one. In the end, his reasons for doing what he is now doing, and believing in its worth, are little different from his reasons for pursuing

29

pleasure as an adolescent and business success as a younger adult – it makes him feel good. Crassly put, he did his thing then, he is still doing his thing now.

An outsider might, of course, point out that, in terms of the overall picture, the collective social structure, his present lifestyle and values are more beneficial to the whole than was his past. But that is not, ultimately, his reason for changing his lifestyle and adjusting his priorities. In the end, the justification of his present lifestyle is the same as that which justified his past, idiosyncratic preference. He is doing his thing.

Again, in this, Brian is more typical than deviant in representing our culture. For the most part, we, like him, do not connect our choice of values and priorities to a structure of value beyond personal preference and the comfort of our own inner worlds. In the end, our own reality is the only one that is real and important.

Given all this, one might now ask: How does this adversely affect contemplation? The effect of excessive narcissism on contemplation can be simply stated. When we stand before reality self-preoccupied we will see precious little of what is actually there to be seen. Moreover, even what we do see will be distorted and shaped by self-interest. This can be illustrated with a simple example.

Imagine taking a walk in a beautiful forest on a splendid summer's day. The earth is ablaze with the fire of God and the sights, sounds, and smells are enough to make you want to take your shoes off before the burning bush. But your mind and heart are hopelessly torn and obsessed because you are painfully infatuated with someone who has just rejected you. You will see virtually nothing on this walk, not just of beauty and creation, but nothing at all. You are inside yourself, obsessed with this infatuation, torn by this pain, endlessly trying on past and future conversations, possibilities, and fantasies. For all you are actually seeing, hearing, or smelling of beauty and nature, you could just as profitably be walking in a car park or a rubbish dump. You are locked inside an inner world whose obsessive reality absorbs virtually all of your awareness. The outside world has little power to penetrate that or even to distract you. Reality, for you, has been reduced to the size, shape, and colour of your own inner world.

This image, an obsessed person walking through a scene of beauty and being oblivious to it, illustrates how narcissism is the antithesis of contemplation. It is also an image of our culture's struggle with seeing God in ordinary life. When we are excessively self-preoccupied, we tend to see nothing beyond our own heartaches and problems. Our sense of reality shrinks accordingly and it is not then surprising that we have trouble believing in the reality of God since we have trouble perceiving any reality at all beyond ourselves.

2) *Pragmatism*

Few words are as apt to describe our Western way of life and its mindset as is the word *pragmatism*. For many people, the very word is synonymous with Western life, especially with American life.

The term pragmatism comes from the Greek word *Pragma* which means 'business', but also holds connotations of efficiency, sensibleness, and practicality.

Simply defined pragmatism is a philosophy and a way of life that asserts that the truth of an idea lies in its practical efficacy. What that means is that *what is true is what works*. The test for truth is not whether an idea corresponds to the way things are in fact in reality, but whether that idea has some concrete utility, whether it has practical consequences, and whether or not it can be used actually to manipulate the world beneficially. Worth lies in achievement. Things are good if they work, and what works is considered good. These ideals of pragmatism lie at the very heart of the Western mind, undergird our technological society, are deeply enshrined in our educational systems, and are evident in our impatience with anything (or anybody) that is not immediately practical, useful, and efficient. In the Western world, what is good and true is what works! Value lies in being practical.

Much of this, of course, is good. There can be no dispute that many things within our modern world which have helped to make life better – medicine, travel, technological advances, and communications – are largely the result of pragmatism. It is not honest to enjoy the benefits of these things and unqualifiedly criticise the philosophy and way of life that produced them. However, with that being admitted, it is important to recognise that pragmatism brings with it, along with its good, some debilitating side-effects. What are these?

i) Since value lies in achievement we tend to take our sense of worth from what we do rather than from who we are.
If we take the pragmatic principle *what's good is what works*, it can become true in reverse: you are only good if you work ... and you are only as good as the work you do. Those equations wreak havoc within our lives.

Psychologists assure us that happiness depends largely upon having a healthy self-image. We are happy when we feel good about ourselves and we are not happy when we do not. In a pragmatic society, unfortunately, we feel good about ourselves only when we are achieving, producing, and contributing in a pragmatic way. What this means is that we feel good and important when we do things that society values as good and important and we feel useless and unimportant when we do things that society does not value in the same way. We hand out admiration and respect, both to ourselves and to others, on the basis of pragmatic achievement more so than on any basis of moral virtue or quality of personality. In a pragmatic society *doing* counts for everything, *being* counts for nothing.

The effects of this make themselves felt everywhere: the achievement of professional goals takes precedence over family life, personal virtue, and leisure; persons who are retired, unemployed, or at home with children, feel unfulfilled and useless; we have no place for handicapped persons, for the aged, for the sick; we sacrifice everything to achieve the ideal professional resume (since we know that our value in society's eyes, and in our own, depends upon it); we end up as part of the rat race, with no time, no leisure, high blood pressure, and a diminished sense of enjoyment, and do not know how we got there or how to get away from that pressure; and, finally, when doing is everything and being is nothing, we end up with nothing helping prepare us for death, for letting go, since our ability to produce is our meaning and so we must cling to our careers and occupations as if they were life itself.

ii) Since thought is for problem-solving, we have little patience for ideas that are impractical

In a pragmatic world, the purpose of human thought is instrumental. Ideas are meant to help us adapt more comfortably to a hostile environment. Consequently, in the Western world we learn as a means, not as an end. Education is more about learning skills for life than it is about learning wisdom for its own sake. Our education systems, research grants, and the overall approach we take to learning reflects this priority. We spend more money in the West doing research on developing better rubber for our car tyres than we spend on researching why teenage suicide is the second leading cause of death among young people today in the Western world. Technology is developing at a rate that staggers our capacities to cope with the novelties it produces and, at the same time, we cannot find ways to live together within our marriages, communities, countries, and within the world as a whole. The priorities in education that a pragmatic culture sets for itself are proving very useful in helping to create the good life but are proving less useful in providing the values we need to share it equitably and amiably with each other and in giving our children reason to even want to live.

iii) Since thought is pragmatic in purpose, the scientific method alone is trustworthy

When the purpose of thought is to be able pragmatically to manipulate things for the benefit of humanity, then the scientific method takes centre stage and, eventually, takes the whole stage as well. In such a pragmatic society, science alone is given the right to establish the facts. Its findings are considered objective. What is proposed by other disciplines, with a different method of knowing – metaphysics, philosophy, mysticism, poetry, or theology – is considered to be purely subjective, a matter of personal faith and blind option. Thus, for example, no one, professional scientist or lay person, has ever seen an atom. Yet, none of us doubt its existence. Science not only assures us that atoms do exist, it positively manipulates them to create nuclear energy. Who can doubt their existence? Likewise, no one, professional mystic or lay person, has ever seen God in this world. Yet, we doubt God's existence despite the fact that mystics assure us of that reality and we see in the lives of many believers (not even to mention Christ, Buddha, and Mohammed) fairly concrete evidence that they are experiencing something real in what they claim as an experience of God. They too, like the scientists, are splitting atoms which release energy. However, in a technological society, we see and understand only one kind of energy, pragmatic. This reduction, as we shall see later, is a debilitating impoverishment.

Much of that impoverishment has to do with a reduction in our contemplative abilities. How does pragmatism adversely influence contemplative awareness?

Thomas Merton was once asked by a journalist what he considered to be the leading spiritual disease of our time. His answer surprised his interviewer. Of all the things he might have suggested (lack of prayer, lack of community, poor morals, lack of concern for justice and the poor) he answered instead with one word, efficiency. Why? Because, he continued, 'from the monastery to the Pentagon, the plant has to run ... and there is little time or energy left over after that to do anything else.' What Merton is pointing out here is that, regarding God and religion, our problem is not so much badness as it is busyness. Simply put, we are not very contemplative because the demands of our lives absorb all of our energies and time.

A recent cover story in *Time Magazine* was entitled 'The Rat Race, How America is Running Itself Ragged.'[4] The article points out how time has become the most precious commodity within today's world, how parents have to make appointments in order to spend time with their own children, how technology has increased the very heartbeat of today's generation, how for many persons the demands of remaining on top of their careers take all of their time and energy, and how people are phoning offices to complain because the office's fax line is busy! The article suggests that the most overt symptoms of all this hurry and pressure caused by the demands of the workplace (physical burnout and addiction to alcohol or drugs) are not its most insidious effects. Rather, all this pressure, it submits, is causing people to grow more restless, less patient, and unable to concentrate on anything for very long. Because we are so busy what happens is that, when we do have leisure, we can only spend it doing something mindless and distracting. There is no energy for anything else.

The effect of all this on contemplation is obvious. There is simply no time or energy (or, at a point, even the capacity) to pray or be contemplative. The expression 'caught in the rat race' says it all. As the *Time* article puts it, 'with too little time for sleep there is also too little time for dreams.'

Beyond this obvious effect on contemplation, one can perceive a more subtle manner in which pragmatism works against contemplation. When self-worth depends upon achievement then very few persons are going to spend much time in prayer or contemplation since these are by definition non-utilitarian, pragmatically useless, a waste of time, a time when nothing is accomplished. One of the major reasons why we are not more contemplative, why we do not pray more, and why we do not take time to smell the flowers, is that these activities do not accomplish anything, produce anything, or practically add anything to life. We feel good about ourselves when we are doing useful things. Contemplative activity, by definition, is pragmatically useless.

We have little time for what is useless and, for that, we are contemplatively the poorer. Caught up as we are in the efficiency demanded by a pragmatic culture, we most often end up like the persons who refused the king's invitation to come to the wedding banquet in Christ's parable.[5] The persons who were excluded did not turn down the invitation because they were impious, irreligious, or morally lax. In fact, they did not turn down the invitation explicitly at all. They simply never showed up, given that they were so busy buying oxen, getting married, and measuring land. In pragmatism, contemplation dies, not through badness, but through busyness.

3) *Unbridled restlessness*
Perhaps no one word so captures the dominant feature and feeling of our culture as does the word restlessness. We are a restless people.

Restlessness is not difficult to define. It is the opposite of being restful. Restfulness is one of the most primal of all cravings inside us. We crave rest to the point where we often identify it with heaven: 'Grant us eternal rest'.

Today, as our lives grow more pressured, as we grow more tired, and as we begin to talk more about burnout, we fantasise more about restfulness. We imagine it as a peaceful quiet place; us walking by a lake, watching a peaceful sunset, smoking a pipe in a rocker by the fireplace. But even in those images, we make restfulness yet another activity, something we do, something we are refreshed by ... and then return to normal life from.

Restfulness, though, is a form of awareness, a way of being in life. It is being in ordinary life with a sense of ease, gratitude, appreciation, peace, and prayer. We are restful when ordinary life is enough.

Thomas Merton, journaling during an extended period of solitude, once wrote:

> It is enough to be, in an ordinary human mode, with one's hunger and sleep, one's cold and warmth, rising and going to bed. Putting on blankets and taking them off, making coffee and then drinking it. Defrosting the refrigerator, reading, meditating, working, praying, I live as my fathers have lived on this earth, until eventually I die. Amen. There is no need to make an assertion of my life, especially so about it as mine, though doubtless it is not somebody else's. I must learn gradually to forget program and artifice.[6]

Today, nothing seems enough for us. The simple and primal joys of living, those Merton describes, are mostly lost as we grow ever more restless, driven, compulsive, and hyper. Within our lives there is less ease, and more fever; less peacefulness, and more obsessive activity; less enjoyment, and more excess. These are the telltale signs of unbridled restlessness.

But have we not always been restless? Are we not pilgrims on earth, built with hearts made for the infinite, caught up in very finite and limited lives? Should we be surprised that we are constantly tormented by the insufficiency of everything attainable? To be hopelessly restless proves little more than that we are alive, emotionally healthy, and normal. Has not God built us so that we are restless until we rest in God?

Restlessness is normal. However, it is like body temperature, beyond a point it becomes an unhealthy fever. Today, for reasons we will examine later, our psychic temperature has risen to become a fever. Our restlessness is excessive. A healthy restlessness pushes us to be healthily dissatisfied with the limits of this life, but restlessness becomes unhealthy when, as Merton puts it, it is 'no longer enough to be in an ordinary human mode, when we must make an assertion of our lives.'

In Western culture today our restlessness is pushing us beyond what is healthy. Consequently three factors impact adversely on our ability to be contemplative:

i) Greed for experience

When restlessness is excessive it is no longer possible to be satisfied with being just a human being ('with one's own hunger and sleep, cold and warmth, making coffee and drinking it.') What is simple and primal, the feel of one's own body and the taste of one's own coffee, is lost in an obsessive greed for experience.

Scholastic philosophy used to say that the adequate object of human yearning is all being in so far as it is knowable and good. That is a rather abstract way of saying that what would ultimately satisfy us would be if we could experience everybody and everything, and be experienced by everyone and everything. Our bodies, minds, and hearts are greedy for experience.

When restlessness becomes excessive then this greed for experience, which normally healthily underlies and motivates all of our actions, begins to drive us outward so that our actions do not issue forth from some free centre, but from compulsion. Our lives become consumed with the idea that unless we somehow experience everything, travel everywhere, see everything, and are part of a large number of other people's experience, then our own lives are small and meaningless. We become impatient with every hunger, every ache, and every non-consummated area within our lives and we become convinced that unless every pleasure we yearn for is tasted, we will be unhappy.

In this posture of unbridled restlessness, we stand before life too greedy, too full of expectations that cannot be realised, and unable to accept that, here, in this life, all symphonies remain unfinished. When this happens an obsessive restlessness leaves us unable to rest or be satisfied because we are convinced that all lack, all tension, and all unfulfilled yearning is tragic. Thus, it becomes tragic to be alone; to be unmarried; to be married, but not completely fulfilled romantically and sexually; to not be good-looking; or be unhealthy, aged, or handicapped. It becomes tragic to be caught up in duties and commitments which limit our freedom, tragic to be poor, tragic to go through life and not be able to taste every pleasure on earth and fulfil every potential inside us. When we are obsessed in this way it is hard to be contemplative. We are too focused on our own heartaches to be very open and receptive.

ii) Impatience and lack of chastity

Some years ago, before the demise of communism in the Soviet Union, I was involved in a bizarre incident that helped highlight, for me, our culture's struggle with patience. I was journeying to the USSR with a group of Western tourists. We arrived in Moscow on a blizzardy December evening, entered the airport, cleared customs, and moved towards our connecting flight to St Petersburg. Then, for reasons never explained to us, we were made to wait ... wait for twenty-four hours, without food or explanation.

Hundreds of other people also waited in the airport that night. Everyone was without explanation, but only our group, the Westerners, appeared to be angry and in a panic. We rushed angrily from desk to desk, demanding explanations and phoning embassies. Blood pressures and temperatures ran high and, within our group, there was the constant indignant expression: 'Nobody can do this to us! We don't have to put up with this!'

What was enlightening in this was that, fairly soon, it was clear as to who in that airport was from the West and who was not. All of us from the West were angry, impatient, indignant, and contemptuous. The Eastern Europeans, on the other hand, waited more passively, without anger and impatience. They smoked, played cards, and drank vodka. They, obviously, were used to waiting. Like the rest of the Western tourists, I too was impatient. Twenty-four hours later, again without explanation, our flight to St Petersburg was announced and our vigil was over. Except that it had not been a vigil. From the beginning to the end, we had fought the waiting and seen it as an imposition on our rights. Later, in a more reflective moment, I was able to see in this incident an important lesson.

Simply stated, the lesson is this: just as we rushed about that airport refusing to wait, impatient, convinced that nobody or nothing had a right to deny us what we wanted, so too we rush about our lives refusing to wait for things, refusing to live in any tension, convinced that nobody or no thing has a right to deny us what we want.

The effect of this impatience is the same everywhere. We see it in our economics, in our sexual morality, and in our constant tendency to seize, as by right, what is by nature gift. There is in our culture an inability to wait and, in this impatience, there is a lack of chastity which is severely debilitating *vis-à-vis* contemplation.

Chastity is normally defined as something to do with sex, namely, a certain innocence, purity, discipline, or even celibacy regarding sex. This, however, is too narrow. Chastity is, first of all, not primarily a sexual concept. It has to do with the limits and appropriateness of all experiencing, the sexual included. To be chaste means to experience things, all things, respectfully and to drink them in only when we are ready for them. We break chastity when we experience anything irreverently or prematurely. Irreverence and prematurity are what violate chastity.

Experience can be good or bad. It can glue the psyche together or tear it apart. It can produce joy or chaos. Travel, reading, achievement, sex, exposure to novelty, the breaking of taboos, all can be good, if experienced reverently and at their proper time. Conversely, they can tear the soul apart (even when they are not wrong in themselves) when they are not experienced chastely, that is, when they are experienced in a way that does not fully respect the other, person or object, that is the subject of the experience or does not respect our own integration.

Unbridled restlessness makes us unhealthily impatient for experience and this often takes us beyond the limits of chastity. Greed and impatience push us towards premature and irresponsible experience. This can be very subtle. We do a lot of things which are very innocent in themselves, but which, in the end, violate chastity. Thus, for example, we give in to our children's impatience and demands and allow them every experience they demand ... travel at a very young age, every kind of consumer object, exposure to whatever movies and videos they desire, dating at age twelve, sex at age sixteen

... and then we wonder why they are bored, cynical, and fatigued in spirit at age twenty.

Allan Bloom, commenting on this, submits that lack of patience and chastity leads to 'an eros gone lame'. Speaking, not from any particular religious perspective, but solely from that of a humanist and educator, he asserts that we are born for a high purpose. We are also built for that purpose. We are fired into life with a madness that comes from our incompleteness and lets us believe that we can recover our wholeness through the embrace of another, the perpetuity of our seed, and the contemplation of God. According to Bloom we have trivialised this longing and made it mean something more concrete, something small, something less. For us, the longing is now simply for the good life, success, pleasure, the sweetening of life. At one point, he quotes Plato who, in his *Symposium*, tells of how his students sit around 'telling wonderful stories of the meaning of their immortal longings.' Bloom points out how his own students sit around and tell less wonderful stories of sexual yearnings much more concretely channelled.[7]

At the root of this, according to Bloom, lies the lack of chastity. Speaking outside any consideration of Christian morality, he suggests that it is premature and non-integrative experience, a lack of chastity, which is lobotomising today's soul and dulling its eros. Premature experience, he asserts, is bad precisely because it is premature. The period of nascent yearning is meant precisely for sublimation, in the sense of making sublime, of orientating youthful inclinations and longings towards great love, great art, great achievement. Premature experience is like the false ecstasy of drugs in that 'it artificially induces the exaltation naturally attached to the completion of the greatest endeavors – victory in a just war, consummated love, artistic creation, religious devotion, and the discovery of truth.'[8] Lack of chastity has the effect of draining great enthusiasm and great expectations. These can only be built up through sublimation, tension, and waiting.

Bloom, in illustrating this, shares that in his experience as a teacher he finds that students who have had a serious fling with drugs – and got over it – find it difficult to have enthusiasm and great expectations ... 'it is as though the colour has been drained out of their lives and they see everything in black and white ...

40

They function perfectly well, but dryly, routinely. Their energy has been sapped, and they do not expect their life's activity to produce anything but a living.'[9]

A generation earlier, Albert Camus had already written: 'Chastity alone is connected with personal progress. There is a time when moving beyond it is a victory – when it is released from its moral imperatives. But this quickly becomes defeat afterwards.'[10]

Few things work as militantly against contemplation as do impatience and the lack of chastity it invariably spawns. In fact, patience and chastity are, of themselves, almost a definition of contemplation. The perception and reception of God, as is evident in the pedagogy of the incarnation, are linked to an experience of advent, a period of waiting in tension and a living in chastity so as to let God be God and love be gift.

iii) The loss of interiority

Socrates once commented that 'the unexamined life is not worth living.' Lately, because of restlessness, we have taken to examining our lives less and less.

Within our culture, distraction is normal; contemplativeness, solitude, and prayer are not. Why is this? We are not, either by choice or ideology, a culture set against the interior life. Nor are we, I submit, more afraid of the interior life than past ages. Where we differ from past ages, as we saw when we examined pragmatism, is not in our badness but our busyness. Where we differ from them too is in the degree of our restlessness.

Henri Nouwen describes the restlessness of our contemporary lives as follows:

> One of the most obvious characteristics of our daily lives is that we are busy. We experience our days as filled with things to do, people to meet, projects to finish, letters to write, calls to make, and appointments to keep. Our lives often seem like over-packed suitcases bursting at the seams. In fact, we are almost always aware of being behind schedule. There is a nagging sense that there are unfinished tasks, unfulfilled promises, unrealized proposals. There is always something else that we should have remembered, done, or said. There

41

are always people we did not speak to, write to, or visit. Thus, although we are very busy, we have a lingering feeling of never really fulfilling our obligations....

Beneath our worrying lives, however, something else is going on. While our minds and hearts are filled with many things, and we wonder how we can live up to the expectations imposed upon us by ourselves and others, we have a deep sense of unfulfillment. While busy with and worried about many things, we seldom feel truly satisfied, at peace, at home. A gnawing sense of being unfulfilled underlies our filled lives.... The great paradox of our time is that many of us are busy and bored at the same time. While running from one event to the next, we wonder in our innermost selves if anything is really happening. While we can hardly keep up with our many tasks and obligations, we are not so sure that it would make any difference if we did nothing at all. While people keep pushing us in all directions, we doubt if anyone really cares. In short, while our lives are full, we are unfulfilled.[11]

Being filled, yet unfulfilled, comes from being without deep interiority. When there is never time or space to stand behind our own lives and look reflectively at them, then the pressures and distractions of life simply consume us to the point where we lose control over our lives.

Furthermore, this lack of interiority is largely the product of undisciplined restlessness. When we are unreflective, invariably it is because our restlessness lacks a proper asceticism and simply propels us into a flurry of activity which keeps us preoccupied and consumed with the surface of life, with the business of making a living, with doing things, with distractions, and with entertainment. It is then that our actions no longer issue from a centre within us, but, instead, are products of compulsion. We do things and we no longer know why. We feel chronically pressured, victimised, and hyper-driven. We overwork, but are bored; socialise excessively, but are lonely; and work to the point of exhaustion, but feel our lives are a waste.

This is the unexamined life as Socrates spoke of it. It is also what Greek mythology had in mind in *the Myth of Sisyphus*.

Sisyphus was a man condemned, for no good reason, to roll a stone up a hill for ever. As soon as it reached the top it rolled back down again and he had to return to the bottom and roll it back up. This is an image of frustration, of having to futilely do an activity which one is powerless to stop. It is also an image of the fruits of a non-contemplative life.

Restlessness, without proper reflection, destroys contemplation and, with it, the sense of God within ordinary life. Why? Because when we operate out of restlessness, rather than out of our true centre, then, in the famous phrase of Augustine, God is within us, but we are outside of ourselves.[12]

'Blessed are the pure of heart, for they shall see God.' What makes our hearts less than pure? As we can see from this analysis, it is not always simply sin, moral laxity, or bad will. Narcissism, pragmatism, and excessive restlessness can muddy our awareness and effectively block us from seeing God within ordinary awareness.

Notes

1) The term 'Yuppie' stands for Young Upwardly-Mobile Persons.
2) Neil Postman, *Amusing Ourselves to Death, Public Discourse in the Age of Show Business*, NY, Penguin Books, 1985, pp. 96–97.
3) Robert Bellah, Richard Madsen, William Sullivan, Ann Swidler, and Steven Tipton, *Habits of the Heart, Individualism and Commitment in American Life*, San Francisco, Harper and Row, 1985, pp. 3–6.
4) Marguerite Michaels and James Willwerth, 'How America Has Run Out of Time' in, *Time Magazine*, 24 April 1989, pp. 48–55.
5) Luke 14:16–24 and Matthew 22:1–14.
6) Quoted by John Howard Griffin, *Follow the Ecstasy*, Fort Worth Texas, JHG Editions, Latitudes Press, 1983, pp. 37–38.
7) Allan Bloom, *The Closing of the American Mind*, NY, Simon and Schuster, 1987, pp. 132–133.
8) *The Closing of the American Mind*, pp. 79–80.
9) *Idem.*
10) Albert Camus, 'A Writer's Notebook', in *Encounter*, Volume 24, No. 3, March 1965, pp. 28–29.
11) Henri Nouwen, *Making All Things New, An Introduction to the Spiritual Life*, NY, Doubleday, 1981, pp. 23–24.
12) Augustine, *The Confession of St Augustine*, X, 27.

Chapter 3

A radically changed situation: the non-contemplative personality

When Nietzsche's madman smashes his lantern in the market-place and announces that God is dead, he wonders how this is possible: 'Who gave us the sponge to wipe away the entire horizon?'[1]

What horizon has been wiped away? The horizon of the contemplative, an horizon within which God is the background to all ordinary experience. However, as we just saw, narcissism, pragmatism, and excessive restlessness can so radically reduce awareness that we no longer see, feel, and think against any horizon beyond our immediate heartaches and headaches.

The end result of this is the emergence in the West of a new personality, one in sharp contrast to the past, and one which might be described as non-contemplative. This non-contemplative personality, which is to a large extent novel within history, is typified by, among other things, seven salient qualities ... all of which stand in stark contrast to the past:

1) *For the non-contemplative, reality holds no dimensions of mystery beyond the empirical. For it, the empirical is the basis of all that is considered valid within human experience*

Basic to the creed of the average person today is the belief that we have already penetrated and unearthed the deepest mysteries of reality in that, although it is admitted and expected that science will perpetually continue to discover new things, we no longer expect science or anything else to discover dimensions of reality beyond what is empirically evident. For

44

most of us, the final spiritual exorcism has already taken place. There are no longer any supernatural dimensions to reality; or, in many cases, even to religion. We no longer expect to find spirit lurking within matter, nor the natural camouflaging the supernatural. There are no mysteries other than empirical ones.

Today's non-contemplative person is not haunted by the scent of unseen roses. For him or her, there is no need to ask the old metaphysical question: 'Why is there something instead of nothing?' Reality is simply there, something one takes for granted. What is real is the empirical, what can be experienced through the senses, and this needs no explanation beyond its immediate empirical causal nexus. Where persons of the past saw an infinite background to any reality or event, there were angels and demons everywhere, the person of today sees reality against a very concrete, empirical, immediate, and pragmatic horizon.

Moreover, as opposed to the person of the past, whose primary focus then was to *wonder at* things, the person of today focuses on things in so far as they have a pragmatic dimension. There is little turning towards reality for non-utilitarian purposes.

For today's non-contemplative person reality is, as in Bertrand Russell's clear words, 'just there, and that's all!' It is a given, something you take for granted. It contains no mysteries beyond its empirical once and one moves towards it more with pragmatic intent than with wonder.

2) *For the non-contemplative nothing is sacrosanct*
Today's person, the non-contemplative, begins with the idea that there are no sacred taboos. Unlike past generations who believed that 'the fear of the Lord is the beginning of wisdom', the non-contemplative believes that exorcism of all fear of the sacred is the true path to knowledge.

Past generations placed a premium on a certain virginity, a certain cautiousness and chastity in experiencing. They believed that there was a certain authority within the very contours of reality which was not to be violated. Thus, certain dimensions of reality carried a mystique (in the deepest sense of that word) which was not to be rendered familiar by indiscriminate experience. That kind of concept, for today's non-contemplative person, smacks of timidity, ignorance, and naivete. The non-contemplative values, above all, experience, every kind of experience. For today's person, there are no taboos stemming from the nature of things themselves, nor are there mysteries and mystiques within reality which are not the result of ignorance or lack of opportunity or nerve in experience. Reality, by and large, is stripped of its mystique, rendered familiar, and seen to possess no dimensions before which human beings must 'take off their shoes' in reverence and respect. For a non-contemplative, the path to truth, to reality, to face-to-face knowledge, lies not in a cautious reserve and respect, but in a rigorous examination, an empirical tasting, which is free of all taboos and hesitations which stem from a sense of sacredness or from a fear of violating reality's natural contours.

In today's non-contemplative atmosphere, naked empirical examination deflates mystique and mystery, and exorcises the sense of the sacred which is, at last, seen as a superstition born of fear. Thus, for example, for past generations, Adam and Eve's eating of the apple (desirable 'for the knowledge it would bring') was seen as a violation of the sacred and as a move antithetical to true knowledge. For today's non-contemplative, this violation of a sacred taboo is the beginning of true wisdom.

The contemplative person of the past was more childlike and radiated a certain innocence bordering on naivete; today's non-contemplative is very adult and radiates a sophistication which borders on the cynical.

Closely connected to this is how these two personalities, the contemplative and the non-contemplative, understand the connection between morality and epistemology.

For the contemplative person of the past the equation between morality and epistemology was formulated this way: all moral self-centredness impedes our ability to know properly. Thus, one should be cautious, reticent, and somewhat scrupulous regarding what taboos one breaks. All selfishness, self-indulgence, lack of chastity, and lack of reverence in experiencing will block purity of heart and distort truth. It will, as it did for Adam and Eve, lead to a certain darkening of the mind.

For today's non-contemplative the connection between morality and epistemology, proper experience and truth, is drawn differently. Indiscriminate experiential testing (and tasting) of knowledge to a large extent replaces chastity, caution, repression, and sublimation as the route to true knowledge. Moreover scientific analysis replaces the old moral absolutes of Christianity and natural law as the exorcist which monitors and purifies awareness. The fear today is not that one might distort experience by being unchaste, but that one might miss out on experience by being uptight. Where past generations feared that lack of chastity would lead to darkening of the mind, the present generation fears that lack of nerve in experience will leave one at a certain infantile level of insight.

3) *For the non-contemplative human metaphysics is the final solution and agnosticism has definite limits*

In opposition to the contemplative who believes that, since God is radically and totally other than ourselves and the reality we know, we can live patiently and believe in God, despite seemingly unanswerable paradoxes, pain, and non-vindicated injustice, today's non-contemplative tends to believe that, since there are inexplicable paradoxes, non-vindicated injustices, and questions which are unanswerable within our present framework, there can be no God ... or, if there is, God is less than fully omnipotent and his metaphysics is similar to ours.

For the contemplative, God's ways are not our ways, his thoughts not our thoughts. There are two sets of rules for reality, one for the finite and another for the infinite. In such a perspective, it is understood that the human mind cannot answer certain questions (evil, predestination, non-vindicated injustice) because the human mind, finite and operating within a finite system of symbols, is by definition too limited ... infinite things cannot be grasped by finite minds.

But this is not the perspective of today. For the non-contemplative mind, in the end, there is only one set of rules for reality, one metaphysics, our own. There is no further framework. Every attempt to render a present problematic situation intelligible by reference to a higher framework (the *mystery* of the God) is seen as ignorance, superstition, or lack of nerve. In such a perspective, there is less reason to contemplate simply because we believe that we already essentially know what there is to know. If there is a God, we already know all about him!

Thus, in opposition to the contemplative whose sense of mystery allows his or her unlimited questioning and possibilities for answers, the non-contemplative questions and examines only in so far as the known empirical possibilities allow. The agnosticism of the non-contemplative is a limited *agnosia*, the questioning and wonder end when the empirically verifiable possibilities are exhausted. In that sense, the non-contemplative does not live his or her life wondering whether the limits of our present perspectives are too narrow and asphyxiating. There is not the constant groping for dimensions beyond the empirical and our present metaphysical possibilities. For the non-contemplative, the function of wonder relates only to empirical mysteries (e.g., Einstein's theories). The theoretical possibility that there might be unseen roses is *a priori* excluded and wonder is given a limited playing field.

4) *The non-contemplative person has a lower symbolic hedge*

As human beings we are distinct from animals on the basis of our symbol-making abilities. We make and use symbols, animals do not. It is symbols that give our actions their meaning. Simply put, our experience means whatever the symbols we use to interpret that experience mean. Hence, experience has depth to the precise extent that the symbols we use to interpret that experience have depth. But this needs explication.

Humans and animals share many common activities. Like us, animals work, live in communities, eat, play, make love, give birth and take care of their young. But, for us, these things, potentially at least, have a far deeper meaning because we enter them differently and surround them with certain symbols. Thus, to use just one example, there are two ways a human being can eat, with symbols or without them.

Often we eat without symbols. Eating then is little different than fuelling up a car. We pull up to the table with an empty tank, quickly and non-reflectively (and without really tasting our food) gulp down a meal and then, like a car pulling back onto the road, we leave the table to return to our busy concerns. We have nourished our bodies, but it has been a non-reflective, rote experience, little different than animal eating.

By way of contrast, we can eat with symbols. Picture this scenario: two persons, deeply in love, set out to dine together. They spend time talking before the meal, perhaps having a drink. Then they approach the table which has been carefully laid out, complete with linen cloths, candles, china and crystal. They hold hands and say a special grace. Then slowly, over the course of some hours, they eat a meal together. They conclude with a toast and a prayer of thanksgiving. In this latter case, much more is happening than simple eating. The eating has been surrounded with a symbolic hedge, with ritual, mystique, aesthetics, romance and providence. This hedge creates a meaning and a depth in the experience that would be absent without it.

Symbols give meaning to life and we, except for our most rote activities, basically always use them to interpret experience. However, symbols are not all the same, some open us up to deeper meaning than others. Thus, again, to offer just one example: imagine a middle-aged man who is bothered by chronic back pains. What, potentially, does this pain mean? It can mean that he has arthritis, a medical symbol; or it can mean he is undergoing some mid-life crisis, a psychological symbol; or it can mean that he is undergoing the paschal mystery, that this is his cross, a religious symbol (or it might mean all three). What is important here is that the symbols with which we enter and interpret our experience can be high or low (the difference between suffering arthritis or being part of the paschal mystery!).

The non-contemplative, unlike the contemplative, tends to live under what both Philip Rieff and Allan Bloom would refer to as a low symbolic hedge.[2] Thus, where the contemplative (of past generations) might refer to his erotic aching as 'immortal longings', the non-contemplative is more prone to speak of 'being horny'; where the contemplative speaks of 'a providential meeting', the non-contemplative is more likely to speak of 'an accident'; where the contemplative speaks of finding a 'soul-mate', the non-contemplative is more prone to speak of 'great chemistry'; where the contemplative speaks of 'being caught up in a painful romance', the non-contemplative is more likely to speak of 'obsessional neurosis', and where the contemplative speaks about human restlessness as 'a nostalgia for the infinite and a sign of being a pilgrim on earth', the non-contemplative is more likely to feel the same discontent and wonder if he needs a career change or a new marriage.

For a non-contemplative, high symbols are, for the most part, considered illegitimate, naive, and in need of exorcism by realism and analysis. The non-contemplative concedes that deep feelings are real, but any interpretation of their significance that exceeds the meaning of sensation is, in the end, unreal. For a non-contemplative, life is to be enjoyed 'without erecting high symbolic hedges around it.'[3] God's absence within ordinary experience, as we will see later, is more than a little connected to the diminished height of our symbolic hedge.

5) *The non-contemplative person no longer connects the 'temple' on earth to the 'temple' in heaven*

In the word 'contemplation' we see the word 'temple' (con/ *templ*/ation). This is significant and not merely an etymological curiosity. The ancients believed that the word 'temple' long before it referred to a building on earth, designated a place in the sky, a certain divine arrangement of the stars, a dwelling for the deities. Part of the root idea then of contemplation was to build on earth something, a temple (a building, your personality, a moral structure), which would correspond with the temple in the sky. Contemplation meant bringing together the two temples, the one in the sky with the one on the earth.

Implicit in this idea of contemplation is the concept of obedience, human life must be brought into conformity with a certain pre-existing divine harmony. Religiously, this was expressed as 'the will of God' and the contemplative spent his or her life searching to find and do God's will. The prototype of sin was seen as, precisely, refusing to genuflect to this will (Adam and Eve and Lucifer disobeying, by saying: 'I will not serve!'). The classical pious gesture of genuflection captures what is implied in this notion of contemplation.

This concept of contemplation as obedience, so evident in the past, is both foreign and largely repugnant to today's personality. There is, for better and for worse, more or less an outright rejection of the concept of obedience to any pre-existing will of God. This is true both within church circles and outside them. Both an understanding of, and the practice of, genuflection have virtually disappeared. This is not by accident. That loss

50

indicates more than a ritual change in piety and liturgical practice. There is something deeper at stake here. Today's personality is simply less aware in ordinary consciousness of God's presence, providence, and demands. If the God of the piety of the past was too demanding, too terrifying, too hung-up on unchanging eternal moral structures and a pre-fab game plan, the God of today is too distant, too uninvolved, too domesticated to merit any adoration.

God, to the extent that he appears at all in the consciousness of the non-contemplative, does not ask for genuflection, nor does he ask that one try to build on earth a temple that matches the one in heaven.

6) *The non-contemplative is work orientated and too busy to go to the wedding banquet*

In the scriptural parable of the wedding banquet, we see that all of the people who were initially invited to the feast ended up missing the banquet. Their failure to show up was due solely to busyness. The feast was going on, but they were too preoccupied with measuring land, testing oxen, and going on honeymoons to take much notice.

This parable is Jesus' own metaphor for non-contemplative awareness. Simply put, agendas get in the way of wonder and pragmatic concerns severely reduce it. When life is dominated by the headaches, pressures, and concerns for making a living, running a household, meeting schedules, and measuring up to the demands of an achievement-orientated culture, then there will be the constant press to manipulate things rather than just to wonder at them. When manipulation of reality replaces wonder at it, then, by definition, there is a reduced awareness. Metaphorically stated, the preoccupation with measuring land and testing oxen reduces the chances of being aware that there is a divinely-initiated banquet going on at the heart of ordinary life.

When Nietzsche asks: 'Who gave us the sponge to wipe away an entire horizon?' one might, with some necessary nuances added of course, answer that a pragmatically-orientated consciousness definitely helps sponge away a good part of that horizon.

7) *For the non-contemplative ordinary awareness is distorted by an unhealthy idiosyncrasy*

We have seen how Western consciousness today is excessively narcissistic, especially in that there is very little sense of the corporate and there is, often, an incapacity for us to motivate ourselves beyond idiosyncratic preference. This narcissism, which marks the non-contemplative person, reduces ordinary awareness in a double way.

First of all, narcissistic heartaches and obsessions become a filter through which we see reality. Reality is seen largely off the mirror of our own ego and its needs. This both distorts and reduces reality in that wonder and the gaze of admiration give way to distortion and manipulation. Allow me to illustrate that with just one example.

James Joyce, in *A Portrait of the Artist as a Young Man*, powerfully depicts the difference between the sheer gaze of admiration that marks contemplative, aesthetic awareness and the gaze of narcissism that marks distorted, manipulative, and lustful awareness. He describes a young man walking down a beach one day and seeing a very beautiful, young, partially-clad girl bathing in the sea. Initially the man's reaction is typical of a young, hormonally charged, male. He ducks into the rocks to get a good look. But he has an extraordinary experience. Instead of feeling lust, instead of all kinds of possessive fantasies and sexual fantasies invading his awareness, he is aware only of this girl's absolute beauty. He simply gazes and admires. There is no longing to possess her, there are no sexual fantasies, there is only awe at beauty.

That gaze of sheer admiration is rare. Normally, our narcissism distorts and reduces that of which we are aware. Our heartaches, obsessions, our emotional and sexual neediness, our woundedness, in a word, our narcissism, reduces what we perceive to the size of our own ego, with its many needs, and colours what we see according to those needs.

Beyond that more obvious non-contemplativeness, narcissism also reduces awareness by falsely enhancing our perception of ourselves as individuals to the point where we incorrectly perceive ourselves as *independent* when in reality we are radically and organically *interdependent* with others and the cosmic world. In the non-contemplative person there is little sense of that, little sense of the corporate, of radical connectedness, of Bell's theorem,[4] of reality as being somehow all of one piece, of the Body of Christ.

The heartaches that result from the idiosyncratic preference, no less than the headaches that result from the pressures of a pragmatic agenda, help sponge away the huge horizon and, consequently, a sense of God is generally absent within ordinary consciousness. To the extent that God is given any place at all within human awareness that place is very limited and specified, namely, in our churches and in explicit religious activity. Here, in church and within explicit religious activity, with some effort, we can make ourselves aware of God's presence, but there is no longer a spontaneous contuition of God within ordinary experience.

Commentators have employed various metaphors to describe this: faith is a hangover, the eclipse of God, the silence of God, living in God's shadow, religion as a nostalgia, God as a guilt neurosis, faith as lack of nerve, religion as a universal obsessional neurosis, God as a calling card.[5] These metaphors, irrespective of whether they are proposed by atheists explaining why some remnents of belief still exist or by believers who are suggesting why our experience of God is so limited, all, in the end, suggest one thing – God is not vital, or important, in ordinary experience. As Nietzsche suggested already a hundred years ago, God is dead in ordinary consciousness. He still lives on the fringes, in our churches, but, even there, his days are numbered.

What this book is suggesting is that this is essentially true, not because God does not exist to be experienced, but because, today in Western culture, we have a very reduced experience. God is present to us but we are no longer present to God because we are no longer contemplative. We have atrophied contemplative muscles. Our contemplative faculty, like a limb that has been immobilised in a cast for a long time and is now healed and healthy but unable to function without rehabilitation, needs exercise and therapy. Or, to vary the metaphor, like a weightlifter who has overdeveloped certain muscles to the detriment of others and has in this way distorted his natural body, we, in Western culture, have over-focused on one part of our consciousness, and neglected another to the point where our natural consciousness, like the weightlifter's body, is distorted. Our contemplative muscles have been under-used and have, as a consequence, atrophied. They need exercise.

God is no longer present in ordinary awareness because ordinary awareness is no longer contemplative. We are living the unexamined life and its price is a practical atheism. The thesis of this book is that this practical atheism is overcome by contemplative awareness. God will be present in ordinary experience when ordinary experience is fully open and not reductionistic.

With this as the background, the second half of this book will examine three major contemplative traditions within Western Christianity and suggest that in their recovery lies the recovery of a vital sense of God within our lives. Agnosticism and atheism (as well as all distorted religious belief) are ultimately a fault in contemplation.

However, before moving on to examine the major contemplative traditions within Western Christianity and the *praxis* for their recovery, it is valuable here, as a contrast to the non-contemplative personality, to define somewhat more precisely what is meant by the term 'contemplation'.[6]

Contemplation, as the term is used here, has four major connotations: i) it implies an *experiential knowledge*; ii) it implies *direct contact* with someone or something; iii) it is a *form of obedience*, a bringing of one's life into conformity with God; and iv) it is *an experience of reality in a way that is not reduced, distorted, or manipulated through narcissism or pragmatism*. In brief, contemplation is 'seeing face to face', without the 'glass, reflecting darkly'.[7]

There are four features contained within this generic definition that need to be further explicated:

1) *Contemplation reveals the extra dimension of reality*

Tertullian once said: 'If I give you a rose you will not doubt God any more, but, of course, the rose has to unlock a mystical insight and appreciation.'[8] When we perceive reality in a non-pragmatic, non-manipulative, and admiring way, we are contemplating it. When reality is allowed to be all that it is and the human mind is allowed to experience it in that way, we become haunted by the scent of unseen roses and the aesthetic, religious, poetic, romantic, ironic, and humorous dimensions within ordinary reality leap to the fore.

As well, when reality is perceived contemplatively, there is a fundamental shift in our attitude towards it. From a wondering *how* and a wondering *whether*, legitimate as these are in themselves, there now begins a wondering *at*. When we begin to wonder *at*, the door to the invisible begins to open and we sense a previously unperceived depth within ordinary reality. When reality is met contemplatively, a contuition of God in ordinary experience is not only possible, it is natural and spontaneous.

2) *Contemplation changes the subject*
Contemplation brings about a certain union with God, others, and the cosmic world. This meeting and undergoing of the presence of the other radically changes the person entering into it. Classical spiritualities had already pointed this out with their submission that all contemplation is purifying, purging, and enlarging of the subject entering into it. Contemporary spiritualities, drawing on new insights taken from psychology and sociology, corroborate this and add further nuances to it. Contemplation changes its subject in six interpenetrating ways:

i) It purifies awareness within the subject
Contemplation is genuine union with others. This union then becomes a light which shows us our idiosyncrasies, our fantasies, our dishonesties, and our selfishness. The experience of unity helps break unhealthy narcissism. As a result, contemplation cuts the roots of our sin. One cannot be in a genuine communion with reality and be wrapped in dishonesty, fantasy, and selfishness. Genuine union is incompatible with these and genuine union is what breaks these. It is for this reason that classical spiritual writers state that, in its initial state, contemplation is always a very painful experience.

ii) It enhances the individuality of its subject
In some Eastern religions, radical union within community (divine, human, cosmic) is understood as swallowing up individual subjectivity. Contemplation, as it has been and is today understood in the Western Christian tradition, suggests the opposite. Far from limiting or eliminating individual self-consciousness,

contemplative union (and all other genuine unity) enhances it. Individuality, as recent sociology and psychology agree, is not incompatible with communion but is rather dependent upon it. Individuality is enhanced proportionately with entry into communion. Conversely, lack of community eventually destroys self-identity. Contemplation, therefore, changes its subject in that it deepens self-awareness.

iii) It makes the subject less pragmatic
One of the direct effects of contemplation is that wondering *how* changes to wondering *at*. Contemplative union then brings to birth admiration, the sheer enjoyment of beauty without the urge to possess it, manipulate it, or assimilate it. Meeting the other in genuine union reduces the pragmatic urge.

iv) It restores to its subject the child's natural instinct for astonishment
A child is a natural contemplative, constantly wondering *at*. For children, everything is laden with aesthetic and supernatural dimensions. Only later, when we approach reality with more and more *a priori* filters, do we begin to see less and less of the aesthetic and the supernatural.

As an illustration, G. K. Chesterton describes the simple phenomenon of an egg hatching into a baby chick. For an adult, this is a very ordinary, mundane thing, the simple outcome of a deterministic and uninteresting law. For a child, or a contemplative, it is magic, a wonder, a miracle, creation itself. The adult describes it in terms of 'law', 'necessity', 'everyday and ordinary', 'order', and the like. The child prefers not to use language at all, he or she is too awe-struck. But the words the child uses suggest magic and miracle, 'God made this', and so on. The adult greets the event with boredom, perhaps even with cynicism; the child greets it with unabashed excitement.[9]

Contemplation has the effect of restoring to the subject the child's instinct for astonishment. This, however, does not mean that the adult returns to the naivete of a child. The critical faculty is not bypassed or denigrated by contemplative awareness. Rather it is stretched and opened even further so that what was formerly seen as a healthy agnosticism and limit in knowing is now viewed as a temporary fixation at a certain level of development. Contemplation restores wonder not by bypassing the critical faculty, but by helping bring on a 'second naivete',[10] a post-criticalness, where as T. S. Eliot says:

> We shall not cease from exploration
> And the end of all our exploring
> Will be to arrive where we started
> And know the place for the first time.[11]

Given this fact, that contemplation restores to its subject the instinct for astonishment, it follows that contemplation is natural to the human person. It is not something we must learn, but something we must relearn, and relearn again, throughout our lives.

v) It increases knowledge and opaqueness at the same time
In contemplative perception, as the range and clarity of vision progressively increase, the obscurity and impenetrability of its background likewise increases. In street language, what this means is that as we learn more we also learn how much we do not know and how much there still is to learn about what we know. In the words of John of the Cross, 'we begin to understand more by not understanding than by understanding.'[12] Precisely to the degree that we begin to see things clearly, our knowledge becomes deeper, darker, and ever more ineffable.

vi) It enlarges its subject
What is implied by this? Concomitant with all ordinary perception is a certain longing or nostalgia for unlimited being, unlimited knowing, and unlimited love. Our own personalities and experience, always, seem too small and asphyxiating to us. We long to be part of everything that is and to have everything that is be part of us. This desire, for union with all that is, to have our personalities co-extensive with all that is, is realised, in a certain fashion, in the union that contemplation brings about. Through contemplative perception, in standing before reality naked and letting reality be for us all that it is in itself, we allow reality into our lives in such a way that it becomes part of us and we part of it. It is through this type of union (rather than through our frenzied attempts to be everywhere at the same time through fame, travel, excessive activity, gluttonous

experience, and monumental achievement) that our personalities become co-extensive with all that is. In contemplation, the torment of the insufficiency of everything attainable, the pain of our own lives never being enough for us, is overcome.

Before this brief digression on what contemplation is and what its salient features are, I suggested that atheism, agnosticism, and distorted religion are, in the end, the result of a fault in contemplation. God will be present in ordinary experience when ordinary experience itself is optimally open and not reductionistic. When ordinary perception is contemplative there will be a contuition of God.

Thus the problem today of unbelief among believers, of God's disappearance from ordinary experience, is a problem with contemplation. The eclipse of God is the eclipse of contemplation. A reduced awareness is the sponge that wipes away an entire horizon. From this, it follows that the road beyond lies in a recovery of our contemplative sense. When we recover our capacity to be astonished within ordinary experience we will again be astonished.

In 1746, Denis Diderot, echoing the creed of the Enlightenment, proposed the following challenge to believers: 'If the religion that you announce to me is true, its truth can be demonstrated by answerable arguments. Find these arguments. Why pursue me with prodigies, when a syllogism serves to convince me?'[13]

Centuries later, comedian Woody Allen remarks: 'I am plagued by doubts. What if everything is an illusion and nothing exists? In that case I definitely overpaid for the carpet. If only God would give me some clear sign; like a large deposit in my name at a Swiss bank.'[14]

The thesis of this book radically disputes that the road to the experience of God lies in syllogisms ... or in the type of miracle that Woody Allen proposes (and which is, less humorously, held up in some fundamentalistic circles as a true theistic apologetic). God is not found at the conclusion of a syllogism, nor on the basis of miraculous interventions within ordinary life, but in living a certain way of life.

Blessed are the pure of heart, the contemplatives, they shall see God. The existence of God, like the air we breathe, need not be proven. It is more a question of developing good lungs to meet it properly. A proper contemplative posture develops these lungs. In contemplation, like Mary pondering the word of God until she becomes pregnant with God's spirit, we gestate the conditions within which God is met, undergone, and celebrated. The road beyond atheism, agnosticism, and distorted religion lies in contemplation.

Contemplation, however, is not a simple phenomenon, nor is it a simple practice that we can achieve on the basis of a weekend workshop and the subsequent practice of a certain technique. It is a whole way of life that involves every dimension of our personalities (moral, spiritual, psychological, emotional, physical, sexual, aesthetic) and every dimension of our lives (private and social).

What follows is a brief sketch of three such contemplative traditions (or, more accurately perhaps, contemplative spiritualities) as they have existed and do exist within Western Christianity. These traditions do not pretend to provide the type of syllogisms that scepticism demands. Nor do they promise miracles. What they do promise is that, at the end of a long journey towards optimal openness, a journey that ultimately demands conversion in every dimension of our personality, God will spontaneously be part and parcel of our ordinary awareness.

Notes

1) F. Nietzsche, *The Gay Science*, NY, 1974, Book 3, no. 125, pp. 182ff.
2) Allan Bloom, *The Closing of the American Mind*, pp. 132–133 and 381. Philip Rieff, *The Triumph of the Therapeutic*, p. 23.
3) Philip Rieff, *The Triumph of the Therapeutic*, p. 23.
4) A theory which complements relativity that John Bell, following Einstein, formulated in 1965 and which has since received a fairly general acceptance in physics. The theory (which deals with statistical correlation) does not easily lend itself to popular explanation but what it seems to indicate is that, at the sub-atomic level, two disparate and non-contiguous entities will manifest, despite immense differences, some very curious similarities which render themselves intelligible only if we postulate that somehow reality is all of one piece.
5) These metaphors have a variety of sources: 'faith as a hangover', John Shea; 'Eclipse of God', Martin Buber; 'Silence of God', I. Bergman; 'Living

under God's shadow', F. Nietzsche; 'God and religion as neurosis and guilt', S. Freud and many Neo-Freudians; 'God as calling card', Philip Rieff.

6) A brief history of the term *contemplation* is valuable in explicating its meaning:

i) In the Old Testament, there is a Hebrew word *da'ath* which connotes an intimate knowledge of something which involves your whole person.

ii) In the New Testament this concept is rendered in the Greek by the word *gnosis*, which designates an experiential knowledge, a certain intimacy (like sexual intercourse), a radical face-to-face presence of one thing to another.

iii) In the early Greek Christian writers (e.g., Clement of Alexandria, Origen, and Gregory of Nyssa), the word *theoria* (a term borrowed from the Neoplatonists) was used to render the meaning of gnosis as well as designate some added connotations. In Neoplatonic philosophy, the term *theoria* referred to an intellectual vision of truth which the mind could contemplate ('theorise'). Thus, the idea of contemplative wisdom was added to the notion of intimacy, immediacy, and experience in knowledge.

iv) In the Latin writers this was rendered by the term *contemplatio*. To the connotations given earlier some additional ones appeared in the Latin conception of this. The very word con/*templ*/ation contains the word *temple*. For the ancients, the temple was, before it was the place where God was worshipped on earth, a place where god(s) lived in the sky. The idea of worship, contemplation, then included the idea of bringing life on earth into conformity with what it was in the sky ('on earth as it is in heaven'). Hence, contemplation took on some connotations of obedience as well. This tradition was summed up by Gregory the Great in the sixth century when he described contemplation as a knowledge of God that is impregnated with love.

v) Later on in the Western mystical tradition *contemplation* will also come to designate something distinct from *meditation*. This distinction is drawn differently within different traditions (e.g., the Carmelite and the Ignatian) and probably dates to Hugo of St Victor (d.1142) who regarded *contemplatio* as the third and final stage of knowledge in the soul's ascent to unity with God ... he had stated that before this stage of *contemplatio* the soul must first pass through *meditatio* which is a stage of preparation for unity.

See: Thomas Keating, *Open Mind, Open Heart*, NY, Amity Press, 1986, especially chapters 2 and 3; David Steindl-Rast, *Gratefulness the Heart of Prayer*, NY, Paulist Press, 1984, especially chapter 5, 'Contemplation and Leisure'; and the article on 'contemplation' in *Dictionary of Philosophy and Religion*, edited by W. L. Reese, NJ, Humanities Press, 1980, p. 105. For a less technical account of this, but one which defines the essence of contemplation magnificently, I recommend a popular book by James Finley, *The Awakening Call*, Notre Dame, Ind., Ave Maria Press, 1984.

7) 1 Corinthians 13:12–13. The literal Greek translation reads: 'For now we see as through *an enigma* (en enigmati)'.

8) Quoted by L. Weatherhead, *The Christian Agnostic*, NY, 1965, p. 77.

9) G. K. Chesterton, *Orthodoxy*, London, 1909, pp. 90–92.

10) Paul Ricoeur is generally given credit for formulating this phrase, though my usage of it will not always and everywhere be identical with his.

11) T. S. Eliot, 'Little Gidding', in, *Four Quartets*, London, 1971, p. 59.

12) This is not a direct quote from John of the Cross, but captures, in a caption, the paradox which lies at the essence of his teaching on contemplative knowledge. This idea of 'dark understanding', i.e., understanding beyond words, concepts, and imaginative constructs, is everywhere present in his works. However for more specific expressions, see: *The Ascent of Mount Carmel*, Book II, chapter 4, number 2; and chapters 6–12 of the same book.

13) Quoted by Michael Buckley, *At the Origins of Modern Atheism*, p. 208.

14) Quoted by R. McAfee Brown, *Is Faith Obsolete*, Philadelphia, 1974, p. 86.

Part II

Recovering the ancient instinct for astonishment:
three contemplative traditions within
Western Christian thought

Chapter 4

The purification of awareness: the mystical tradition

MYSTICISM AS A WAKING UP

In his autobiography, *Report to Greco*, Nikos Kazantzakis tells how as a young man he went to visit a then-famous monk. He describes this encounter as follows:

> Working up courage, I entered the cave and proceeded toward the voice. The ascetic was curled up on the ground. He had raised his head, and I was able in the half-light to make out his face as it gleamed in the depths of unutterable beatitude. . . .
>
> I did not know what to say, where to begin. . . . Finally I gathered up courage.
>
> 'Do you still wrestle with the devil, Father Makarios?' I asked him.
>
> 'Not any longer, my child. I have grown old now, and he has grown old with me. He doesn't have the strength. . . . I wrestle with God.'
>
> 'With God!' I exclaimed in astonishment. 'And you hope to win?'
>
> 'I hope to lose, my child. My bones remain with me still, and they continue to resist.'
>
> 'Yours is a hard life, Father. I too want to be saved. Is there no other way?'
>
> 'More agreeable?' asked the ascetic, smiling compassionately.
>
> 'More human, Father.'
>
> 'One, only one.'

'What is it?'

'Ascent. To climb a series of steps. From the full stomach to hunger, from the slaked throat to thirst, from joy to suffering. God sits at the summit of hunger, thirst, and suffering; the devil sits at the summit of a comfortable life. Choose.'

'I am still young. The world is nice. I have time to choose.'

Reaching out with the five bones of his hand, the ascetic touched my knee and pushed me.

'*Wake up*, my child. *Wake up* before death wakes you up.'[1]

These words, *wake up*, in caption, capture the basic prescriptive counsel of the first contemplative tradition we will be examining, the mystical tradition within Western Christianity.

This tradition of Western mysticism can be summarised in Jesus' words: 'Blessed are the pure of heart, for they shall see God.'[2] According to the great mystics within it, we generally lack the purity of heart necessary to see God because normal awareness is both very reduced and muddied by unhealthy self-concern, excessive preoccupation with our own agendas, and with restless distractions. God is present but we are, for the most part, asleep, distracted, and unaware of that presence. For them, outside certain moral and religious practices which they describe and prescribe, we lack the purity of heart necessary to experience any God that is not one of our own creation. In this tradition, the road beyond practical atheism and idolatry lies in the purification of our awareness, that is, in the purging from our minds and hearts of all unhealthy narcissism, pragmatism, and distraction.

Who represents this tradition? Jesus said that the pure of heart will see God. An explicit tradition developed when, within the first centuries of Christianity, the desert fathers and others took up this challenge, the pursuit of purity of heart, as the object of their monastic quest, and began developing explicit descriptions and prescriptions for a contemplation that they felt would bring about this purity of heart. Their descriptions of contemplation and their prescriptions for it had a strong influence within both Eastern (Greek) and the Western (Latin) Christianity. Countless men and women helped develop this tradition and mediate it down through the centuries, though its expression in the Pseudo-Dionysius around AD 500, helped particularly to crystallise some of its key mystical concepts which then later influenced the great medieval, modern, and contemporary bearers of this tradition, namely, Bernard of Clairvaux, Hildegaard of Bingen, Meister Eckhardt, Jan Van Ruysbroeck, Julian of Norwich, Francis of Assisi, Thomas Aquinas, Bonaventure, John of the Cross, Teresa of Avila, Ignatius of Loyola, Greek and Russian Hesychasm, the Cloud of Unknowing, Therese of Lisieux, and the contemporary bearers of this torch such as Teilhard de Chardin, Catherine de Hueck Doherty, Thomas Merton, Ruth Burrows, and Henri Nouwen.

What do these mystics propose? How do they suggest that we unmuddy our awareness and exercise our contemplative muscles so as to attain the purity of heart that brings about an awareness of God within ordinary consciousness?

At the root of this tradition lies the concept of mysticism. God is *mystically* present within us and around us, but we are not, save for rare moments, aware of that presence. What is implied here?

As it appears in contemporary language, the word mysticism is almost universally misunderstood. For most people it connotes an experience which is esoteric, miraculous in some way, and beyond and against normal experience. Thus we play off mystical experience against ordinary experience. At its best, it is understood as the extraordinary experience of the religious elite, a high road not travelled by normal folk. At its worst, it is placed somewhere on those outer fringes where parapsychology, telepathy, and the occult meet. Rarely is it understood as connoting something to do with ordinary life.

However, as this tradition defines it, mysticism is in fact a very ordinary experience, an experience open to all and had by all. Simply defined, mysticism is being touched by God (or anything else) in a way that is inchoate, namely, in a way that goes beyond what we can think, express, pictorially imagine, and even clearly feel. Mystical knowledge is real knowledge, but it is 'dark knowledge'. We *know it*, but we *cannot think it, express it,* or even *feel it* clearly. In that sense, mystical experience is, by definition, always partly ineffable, dark, inchoate, too huge to properly conceptualise and speak about.

Thus all of us have mystical experience, though not all of us are mystics. Mystical experience is not the high road of the spiritual elite, or the esoteric road of the occult, or the parapsychological road of telepathy. It is the ordinary road for everyone. At his or her depth, everyone is touched, held, and *seared* by God in such a way that, unless one lacks purity of heart, that is, unless one is hardened by sin or drugged by excessive selfishness and distraction, that presence of God will be felt and will progressively swell in such a way that God's reality, goodness, forgiveness, and moral demands will be part of the very colour of one's life, even when one does not, and cannot, explicitly think, imagine, or articulate that presence. If one lives in purity of heart, then God will colour that person's heart, life, and perception, even when that presence is not always part of that person's explicit self-consciousness.

However, as can be seen from this definition, that mystical presence of God depends upon purity of heart, upon being free of unhealthy narcissism, excessive pragmatic concern, and restless distractions. Accordingly, this mystical tradition goes on to spell out how one rids oneself of these. To this end, it begins by making an essential distinction between two things which it terms *praxis* and *theoria*. By *praxis* it refers to all that we can do to dispose ourselves correctly so as to be optimally open and receptive to that mystical presence, namely, acts of meditation, asceticism, religious practice, moral practice, social justice, and duties of state. All of these, in its view, must be done in such a way that the heart remains pure, humble, and unencumbered by excessive selfishness and distraction. The second term, *theoria*, refers to receptivity, to the passive receiving of the presence of God, others, and the cosmic world. In *praxis* the heart correctly disposes itself, in *theoria* the heart receives.

Given this distinction, this tradition then goes on to outline what this *praxis* should consist of so that the kind of purity of heart that one needs to see God might be obtained and then retained. The writings of the great Christian mystics are, in a manner of speaking, detailed descriptions and prescriptions, a *praxis*, for attaining purity of heart.

What is that *praxis*? What are those descriptions and prescriptions? How does one attain purity of heart so that God's mystical presence continually pervades one's consciousness and colours one's awareness with its reality and graciousness? How is human awareness purified from unhealthy narcissism and from the obsessive concerns that issue forth from excessive pragmatism and restlessness? How do we, in the words of Father Makarios to the young Kazantzakis, wake up, before death wakes us up?

The tradition of mysticism, like a diamond that has been cut and polished through many centuries, has too many sides and angles to be taken in simply or seen all at once. One can only walk round it and stare at it from various angles. Given this excessive richness, I have chosen to give it expression here as it is outlined in just one of its major representatives, the Spanish mystic, John of the Cross. Metaphorically stated, we will be looking at only one of its sparkles, though an important and much-venerated one. This expression, that of John of the Cross, has been chosen not because it is considered better or more normative than others, but because of its systematic and synthetic character.

Unlike so many other mystics whose attempt to express their mystical experience does too much justice to the wildness and ineffability of that experience, John, being both an extraordinary poet and exceptional synthetic thinker, has, in a manner of speaking, been able to give left-brained expression to right-brained experience while still protecting the inchoate, dark, ineffable character of that experience. Hence, John of the Cross was chosen because, among mystics, he is exceptional in expressing somewhat the inexpressible. In his writings we find a detailed description of mysticism and clear prescriptions for attaining the purity of heart necessary to be in touch with what is mystically present within us. John presents a systematic paradigm for the purification of awareness.

A PARADIGM FOR THE PURIFICATION OF AWARENESS: THE STAGES OF TRANSFORMATION IN THE SPIRITUAL LIFE ACCORDING TO JOHN OF THE CROSS

1) *John's starting point ... 'Fired with love's urgent longings'*

On 12 February 1944, Anne Frank wrote these words in her now-famous diary:

> Today the sun is shining, the sky is a deep blue, there is a lovely breeze and I am longing – so longing for everything. To talk, for freedom, for friends, to be alone.
> And I do so long ... to cry! I feel as if I am going to burst, and I know it would get better with crying; but I can't, I'm restless, I go from room to room, breathe through the crack of a closed window, feel my heart beating, as if it is saying, 'can't you satisfy my longing at last?'
> I believe that it is spring within me, I feel that spring is awakening, I feel it in my whole body and soul. It is an effort to behave normally. I feel utterly confused. I don't know what to read, what to write, what to do, I only know that I am longing.[3]

This kind of restlessness is what John sees as the impetus that sparks the spiritual journey. He begins his famous poem, 'The Dark Night' with these words,

> One dark night,
> Fired with love's urgent longings ... [4]

For John, just as for Plato and Augustine before him, we are fired into life with a madness that comes from the gods and which leaves us incurably restless, seeking, longing, and insatiably drawn to a beauty, goodness, truth, and unity beyond ourselves. For him, this restlessness is nothing less than a nostalgia for the infinite, a holy eroticism, and a congenital propensity to embrace everything and to become part of everything. Accordingly it creates a perpetual tension at the centre of both our conscious

70

and unconscious lives. We come into life neither restful nor content, but, precisely, fired by love's urgent longing, dis-eased, our souls sick in an advantageous way.

These urgent longings are experienced in many ways, both holy and unholy, during the course of life. Our longing takes as its object many things. Irrespective of that, the ultimate object of that longing is consummation, a complete and ecstatic union with God, others, and the cosmic world. For John, our hearts are restless and they will be restless until they rest in that consummation.

This restless dis-ease, in his view, constitutes the human spirit, the soul, the drive towards life. What we do with it is our spiritual life. If we use this restlessness creatively, to move towards union with God, others, and the cosmic world, then we are living a healthy spiritual life. Conversely, if we do not contain and channel it properly and it leads us to destructive behaviour which takes us away from real union with what is beyond us, then we are living an unhealthy spiritual life. For him, the spiritual life is how we contain, channel, and direct this fire that is within us.

Thus, in John's view, we are built in such a manner and touched by God in such a way that we are incurably sick in an advantageous way. This advantageous sickness, restlessness, is felt as longing, urgent longing, which relentlessly draws us towards goodness, beauty, truth, and union. Ultimately this longing demands that we come into a consummate union with all that is: God, other persons, and the cosmic world. In biblical language, our urgent longings draw us towards seeing face to face.[5]

But are we not already now in a face to face union, at least with others and the world, if not with God? What blocks union in our normal everyday lives?

John would agree with Paul's assessment in 1 Corinthians that 'now we see as through a glass, darkly [an enigma], but then we shall see face to face.'[6] For him, as for Paul, the union we now have with God, others, and the cosmic world is veiled, partially blocked, shadowy, and inconsummate. We see and relate as through a mirror, a riddle, an enigma. What constitutes this blockage?

John throws light on this by employing a metaphor. He suggests that there are three *veils* separating us from full

71

community with God, others, and the cosmic world, three blockages that prevent us from seeing face to face. Each of these veils must, according to him, be stripped by journeying through a *dark night*. Undergoing these dark nights so as to strip away these veils, is, for John, what the spiritual quest is all about. Our urgent longings were given to us precisely so that we might venture outward into this dark night.

Undergoing these dark nights is also, for him, a way of clearing our contemplative vision so as really to see things as they are. John's paradigm for transformation is, first and foremost, about contemplation, about seeing beyond the narcissism, pragmatism, and restless distraction which normally cloud and muddy our vision.

What are the three veils that block us from seeing things as they are and what are the three dark nights through which we must pass? John terms the three blockages *the veil of the senses*, *the veil of the spirit*, and *the veil of life itself* and states that each of these must be stripped away by undergoing a certain dark night.

2) *The transforming process . . . three veils and three dark nights*

i) The dark night of the senses . . . changing our natural motivation

For John of the Cross, we come into this world heavily governed by natural instinct. Initially our dominant instinct is for pleasure. Thus, prior to a spiritual transformation, we are naturally motivated by the desire for pleasure and gratification. This instinctual movement towards what gratifies us constitutes, for him, the *veil of the senses*, a blockage which effectively blocks proper vision and union with what is outside ourselves and it leaves us seeing as through a glass, darkly. How so?

According to John, when we have our own pleasure and gratification as the motivating principle driving our interactions with others then we do not see others as they truly are in themselves. Thus, for example, imagine a baby: does it really see its mother as the mother really is in herself? Obviously not. The baby, at this point of its life, is necessarily tied to instinctual gratification in such a way that it knows and sees the mother primarily as someone who responds to its needs. The mother's own needs, complexities, tiredness, and heartaches are not seen by the baby. The baby sees the mother precisely as through a mirror, reflecting badly, that is, against the mirror of its own need. We might ask the same thing *vis-à-vis* a sexually charged adolescent: is he really seeing the girl that he is looking at (in all her own neediness and complexity) or is he seeing her simply in reflection off the mirror of his own sexual and ego needs?

For John, there is a natural link between instinctual satisfaction and our motivation to act. Put more simply, this means that we spontaneously operate out of the pleasure principle. This, as we just saw, blocks us from seeing others and the world as they really are. For him, this is the veil of the senses.

The *dark night of the senses* is what strips this veil away and purifies us. It does this by severing the spontaneous connection between pleasure and motivation. In the dark night of the senses our motivation is purified: actively, through an immersion into the life of Christ, and passively, through the experience of aridity.

For John, the active part of the night of the senses consists in the deliberate attempt to meditate upon the life and person of Christ and a concomitant effort to begin to appropriate Christ's motivation as the basis of our own action and choice. Put more simply, if one is to motivate oneself beyond the attainment of pleasure and self-satisfaction, one needs a new motivation. In the active night of the senses one studies and meditates Christ's motivation so as to attempt to actively imitate that motivation in one's own life.

The passive part of the dark night of the senses consists in feeling and accepting the experience of dryness and aridity. According to John, God, like a mother weaning a child, dries up the experience of satisfaction and takes away the pleasure we used to receive in prayer and the things of God as well as the pleasure we used to receive from the things of earth. We become, in his words, wearied of both God and creature and are then left with an arid feeling bordering on distaste and disgust. Nothing within prayer or the world any longer gives us the pleasure and satisfaction it once did. Further still, we are left with the painful feeling that we are not serving God and our neighbour properly. We no longer feel, both in our relationship to God and to each other, the enjoyment, good feelings, security, and pleasure we used to feel. In John's view, if we endure and persevere in prayer to God and service to others, despite the absence of all pleasure and satisfaction, then we will begin to act with a new motivation, Christ's, and the spontaneous connection between our own satisfaction and our motivation to act will have been severed. We will then be able to act and to choose not because of the pleasure and satisfaction these bring us but because of something higher, Christ's motivation, namely, a desire to be of help to everything and everybody in their struggle towards consummation and union in love, beauty, truth, and goodness.

This change in motivation will bring with it a new and a purified awareness. Freed from the type of neediness that causes us to project ourselves into everything and onto everybody we see, we will begin to see others and the world more as they are in themselves, with their own uniqueness, beauty, complexity, and need for salvation. New motivation will bring with it new eyesight, new understanding, new empathy. Once we think and feel more like Christ, we will also *see* more like he does. Through the dark night of the senses our awareness is purified of much of the unhealthy narcissism, over-pragmatic fixation, and unbridled restlessness that normally prevents us from seeing anything as it really is. Only after passing through this dark night do we move somewhat beyond manipulation to empathy, beyond reduced vision to wonder, and beyond projection to actually seeing.

But all of this is descriptive. A critical question still remains, the prescriptive one: How do we enter into this dark night of the senses and undergo it properly? John of the Cross gives very clear counsels as to how one enters this night. For the sake of clarity and conciseness we will number them:

1) First, for John, prior to any attempt to enter into the dark night of the senses, or certainly concomitant with it, a certain ascetical, moral, emotional, and psychological discipline is required. What is it? One cannot enter the dark night of the senses, at least not with any seriousness, depth, or staying-power, if there is in his or her life any gross moral laxity, if there is too high a level of psychological depression, or if excessive worldly distraction is constantly drowning out deeper thoughts and voices. As well, entry into the night depends upon regularising one's prayer and liturgical life.[7] Moral laxity and the absence of a prayer life effectively keep one

fixed upon one's own satisfaction and upon pleasure as a motivation for acting. In this way, they limit awareness. Psychological and emotional depression, and even physical sickness, if too severe, tend likewise to keep us focused upon ourselves rather than upon others. Constant superficial distraction tends to block us from even realising the importance of the journey we are invited to make.

Hence, John's first prescription for entry into the night of the senses might be stated as follows: Practise a certain moral and psychological asceticism, have a regularised prayer life, have a certain ecclesial involvement, don't be depressively self-focused, and don't junk up the surface of your life with too many superficial distractions.

2) Next, John gives five prescriptive counsels for active entry into this night:[8]

a) Meditate and study the life and person of Christ.

b) Strive to imitate the motivation of Christ, act and choose for the kingdom of God. Do everything out of a longing to help create a union of minds and hearts so that everything and everyone is helped in their struggle to come to a community of love, beauty, truth, and goodness. Give and receive life in such a way that the life of the trinity can flow through you to everything and everybody you meet.

c) Endeavour to be inclined to be suspicious of yourself and constantly discern your motivation. Be suspicious of what fulfils your natural inclinations, that is, be suspicious when the glory of God and your own glory habitually harmonise. Enter into the vulnerability of Christ, into his unwillingness to protect himself against pain as he fulfils God's will. Make the preferential option for the poor.

d) Relativise what you think about yourself and what others think of you. Move beyond your need for praise, affirmation, recognition, status, and attention. Motivate yourself beyond these. Let yourself be forgotten, counted for nothing.

e) Be patient and loving enough to wait. Do not attempt directly to attain satisfaction, possession, and recognition. Let God justify you rather than attempt self-justification. Through a dialectical process of negation attempt to see things as they are. Hence move by the following guideline:

To reach satisfaction in all
desire its possession in nothing.
To come to possess all
desire the possession of nothing.
To arrive at being all
desire to be nothing.
To come to the knowledge of all
desire the knowledge of nothing.
To come to the pleasure you have not
you must go by a way in which you enjoy not.
To come to the knowledge you have not
you must go by a way in which you know not.
To come to the possession you have not
you must go by a way in which you possess not.
To come to be what you are not
you must go by a way in which you are not.
When you turn towards something
you cease to cast yourself upon the all.
For to go from all to the all
you must deny yourself of all in all.
And when you come to the possession of the all
you must possess it without wanting anything.
Because if you desire to have something in all
your treasure in God is not purely your all.[9]

Thus, John's second prescription for entry into the night of the senses might be summarised as follows: Make an effort to appropriate the motivation of Christ as the basis for all your actions and choices.

3) Finally, John counsels perseverance in aridity and dryness. Passage through the dark night of the senses, at a point, demands that a person accept a period, perhaps a very long one, within which he or she will experience virtually no pleasure or consolation in loving and serving God and others. The person must continue to persevere in prayer, love, and service despite the lack of virtually all gratification.

John's third prescription for entry into and passage through the night of the senses, then, could be put this way: Perseverance in prayer, love, and service, despite feeling no satisfaction in doing these.

For John, the end result of all of this passage through the dark night of the senses, will be a fundamental change in our motivation. Instead of moving out to interact with others and the world because of the gratification, satisfaction, and pleasure they bring us, we will, after this transformation, move out for a much different, and higher, reason, namely, a desire to help everything and everybody in their struggle to come into a genuine community of love, beauty, truth, and goodness. What the dark night of the senses gives us is Christ's motivation.

In the light of this, there will be a fundamental change in our perception: instead of seeing everything and everybody reflected off the mirror of my own ego and its needs, I will see them more as they really are in themselves, in the fullness of their own uniqueness, complexity, beauty, and need for salvation. I will then see beyond the mirror created by my narcissism, my pragmatic concerns, and my restless distractions.

Once this has been accomplished, a major purification of awareness has occurred. There are, however, further blockages, more veils, which still stand in the way of genuine perception and complete unity. Two more dark nights are still necessary, according to John of the Cross.

ii) The dark night of the spirit ... to live in faith, hope, and charity

The *dark night of the spirit* is the second phase of the purification of our awareness. According to John, it is a far more demanding and painful purification than is the dark night of the senses. He calls it the night of faith and says that its purpose is no longer the purification of our motivation, but the purification of what we rely on for knowledge, love, and security. What the dark night of the spirit does is to purify our heads, hearts, and persons in such a way that these now relate to everything, not through their normal propensity for conceptual understanding, possession, and security, but through faith, charity, and hope. More specifically, what does this mean?

77

For John of the Cross, there are three major centres within the human person ('the soul's faculties', he calls them): WILL, INTELLECT, and MEMORY. Although these are linked to various external and internal senses, ultimately, for him, it is through these faculties that we come to know and relate to that which is outside ourselves.

Now, by nature these faculties are hard-wired to work spontaneously in the following way: the INTELLECT (the head) has an incurable need to form concepts and imaginative images and to understand and relate reality to itself through these; the WILL (the heart) spontaneously tries to possess what it loves; and the MEMORY (in contemporary terms, the personality or the ego) has a congenital bent for security, it tries always to control how it relates to reality and how reality relates to it so as to guarantee its own safety. Hence, spontaneously, we guide our lives by conceptual knowledge, possessive love, and a certain control that seeks to guarantee our own security. These mediate our contact with the outside world, partially making that outside world present to us and partially obstructing its presence. Hence, the way our heads, hearts, and personalities spontaneously function creates yet another veil, an enigma, which blocks full communion and full seeing.

How do these natural propensities block vision of and communion with that which is outside us? How do they help create the mirror through which we see badly?

Simply put, when we understand and relate to something *only* in so far as we can intellectually grasp it, and *only* in so far as we can possess it, and *only* in so far as we can remain in control and secure in the face of it, we will be relating only partially to that reality. An image can be helpful in understanding this. Imagine that you have a beautiful photograph of your mother. It is a good photograph; perhaps it even captures her character in a way that is exceptional. That is all true and good, but it is not your mother! Her reality is infinitely larger, richer, and more complex than can be captured in that photograph or a million others. Our conceptual understanding functions similarly. Through the concepts and the imaginative pictures that our heads spontaneously construct, we see each other and the world outside ourselves as we see our mother in a photograph – it is her, but her actual reality dwarfs what is captured in the photograph. The natural bent of the heart for possessiveness and the personality for security, in the end, limit in the same way. Good as these natural propensities are, ultimately, they block true perception and true relationship.

The purpose of the dark night of the spirit is to purify us by opening our heads, hearts, and personalities to a new way of understanding, loving, and relating. Without destroying or denigrating their natural functioning, this transformation stretches the natural capacities of these three faculties to their optimum. Specifically, it transforms them as follows.

The INTELLECT is moved beyond its natural reliance on concepts and images to understand and know through a new type of knowledge, *faith*; the WILL is moved beyond its natural reliance on possessive love to a new type of love, *charity*; and the PERSONALITY (EGO) is moved beyond its natural reliance on security to a new type of reassurance, *hope*.

With this transformation we are, in John's view, opened to a whole new awareness, an awareness that is precisely mystical. However, because our heads, hearts, and egos are not linked in their normal way to what is outside them, this new way of knowing, loving, and relating is, initially, something which is quite painful to us and is felt as a kind of darkness.

How is this transformation accomplished? What causes the head to move from a reliance on concepts to a reliance on faith? What causes the will to move from a reliance on possession to a reliance on charity? And, what causes the personality to move from a reliance on security and control to trusting in hope?

The dark night of the spirit is entered into when one makes the decision to live by raw faith. Like the night of the senses, this night too has both an active and a passive aspect.

Actively, the dark night of the spirit begins when a person concretely makes the choice to guide his or her life, not on the basis of the normal spontaneous functioning of the head, heart, and personality, but, like Abraham who 'set out without knowing where he was going,'[10] on the basis of God's word alone. For John of the Cross, the dark night of the spirit begins when, on the basis of 'the rungs and articles of faith', we begin to think, love and relate beyond the natural movements and instincts of our heads, hearts, and egos. If we, actively, try to understand through faith, love through charity, and relate through hope, God does the rest.

Passively, we then begin to feel the withering of all the understanding, support, and consolation that we used to derive from the intellectual concepts, possessive love, and the control we exercised in our lives. This, according to John, eventually leads to great desolation. We are no longer able to derive any support or guidance from our natural faculties and we then experience inside ourselves a horrible emptiness, a sense of weakness, a feeling of abandonment, and a feeling of being dead ... 'the soul feels that God has rejected it and with an abhorrence of it casts it into darkness.'[11] However, this desolation notwithstanding, our heads, hearts, and egos, deprived of their normal way of relating to what's beyond them, then begin to rely on faith, hope, and charity as the prisms through which they relate.

That brings with it a purified perception, in a surprising number of ways. First, we no longer see things through the medium of the intellectual and the imaginative pictures we create of them. Rather, instead of looking at something through the pictures and icons that our minds create of it, we now look at it in its totality and its wildness. Then, instead of seeing it in terms of possessive love, we now see it more as it exists in itself, in all its richness, complexity, and beauty. The gaze of possessiveness, lust, and jealousy turns into the gaze of admiration, possessive consciousness turns to appreciative consciousness. Finally, instead of allowing the reality of the other into our life only in so far as we can control it and still feel secure, we now let ourselves see and grasp that reality in its fullness, complete with those aspects which we cannot control and which threaten our security. That kind of relating is what constitutes faith, hope, and charity.

However, seeing reality through faith, hope, and charity, does not just change our moral lives. First and foremost, it *changes our eyesight*! When Father Makarios tells the young Nikos Kazantzakis to 'Wake up, before death wakes you up!' it is to this type of waking up that he is referring.

In outlining how this dark night of the spirit purifies our awareness, John is, again, not just descriptive, he is also prescriptive. He gives a very clear counsel on how one is to enter this night and remain in it. For him, the *praxis* required to enter the night of the spirit is reliance upon faith alone. A person must take the articles of faith and use them to concretely cut real life in terms of his or her decisions, choices, and actions: 'Like a blind man he must lean on dark faith, accept it for his guide and light, and rest on nothing of what he understands, tastes, feels, or imagines. All these perceptions are a darkness that will lead him astray. Faith lies beyond all this understanding, tasting, feeling, and imagining. If he does not blind himself in these things and abide in total darkness, he will not reach what is greater – the teaching of faith.'[12]

In summary, John's prescriptive counsel for entry into the dark night of the spirit is: Let the articles of faith, not your feelings and knowledge and need for security, become your guide for living!

For John, once someone has undergone this dark night of the spirit, one has purified his or her awareness to the extent that it is possible in this life. One is now looking at everything and everybody with the eyes of Christ. There is, however, not yet a full face to face seeing of and communion with what is beyond us. One final veil remains to be stripped away, the veil of life itself.

iii) The dark night of death ... coming fully face to face
For John of the Cross, part of what blocks us from seeing face to face is natural life itself. Human nature, of itself, is an impediment to full consummation with everything and everybody. Once a person has undergone the dark nights of the senses and of the spirit, that person is then aware 'that nothing is wanting other than to tear the weak veil of this natural life, in which it feels the entanglement, hindrance, and captivity of its freedom, and since it desires to be dissolved and to be with Christ, it laments that a life so weak and base impedes another so mighty and sublime.'[13]

What is John referring to here? How does natural life itself impede union with God, others, and the world?

One must guard here against an answer that would explain this too simplistically in terms of classical dualism which sees the body as something to be escaped from so that full union in heaven can take place. John is a dualist (in the manner that classical medieval philosophy is dualistic) but the limitations that he is speaking about here, that final bondage that must be stripped away by death, should not be understood in the sense that the soul is pure and can fly but the body is sinful and weighs one down, thus making salvation largely an escape from flesh.

No. For him, while we are in this world our human nature simply limits us, in every way: we can only be at one place at one time; our capacity for love is limited, we cannot be polymorphously loving and sexual, but must choose between monogamy and promiscuity; our capacity for understanding is limited, not just because we see always from a limited perspective, but because we must conceptualise and speak within the framework of a very finite system of symbols; and, in this life, tied to natural instinct and human nature, the human heart and personality simply can never move to the fullness of perception and love. We are, short of death, too incurably human!

Death brings about the final purification, not by making us a-cosmic, angels who no longer have bodies, but by making us pan-cosmic persons, spirits with the entire cosmos for a body. Full perception and entirely purified awareness, for John, require this.

For John of the Cross, in the end, these three dark nights are really one night, one transformative journey which leads by way of a series of reversals, disappointments, sacrifice, and suffering to a radically purified awareness. In this purified awareness, perception becomes much more reception, and movement towards others become more a question of admiration than of manipulation. Once we have been purified through this dark night we stand before reality free from much of the projection and distortion that normally come from the obsessions caused by our narcissism, pragmatism, and unbridled restlessness.

With this purified awareness there also comes a disclosure of God. God is known now through mystical union, in dark knowledge, through understanding more by not understanding than by understanding. This is knowledge in the biblical sense. In this kind of knowledge, one does not intellectually grasp what is going on and, at the level of feeling, does not have the awareness and security that God is real. Rather there is the inchoate sense that our every breath and our every second is being held in existence and guided by a God who cannot be grasped but who can be touched and undergone in love.

It is this, that inchoate mystical sense of God brought about through a purified awareness, that is lacking in the people accused by Nietzsche's madman. When he shouts in the market-place: 'God is dead and we are his murderers!' he is referring precisely to how everyday consciousness can be so preoccupied with the obsessions coming from narcissism, pragmatism, and restlessness that God, in terms of our actual awareness, is in fact dead!

John of the Cross suggests that the God who is dead in this sense can be resurrected through a transformative process called the dark night of the soul, a process which purifies awareness, which, in the words of Father Makarios (not to mention Buddha) 'wakes us up'. In suggesting this, he speaks for the entire mystical tradition.

MYSTICAL PURIFICATION AND THE PURIFICATION OF NATURAL WONDER

When John of the Cross outlined these descriptions of and prescriptions for a transformative dark night, he was writing for persons who were already far advanced in the spiritual journey and for whom the radical question of God's existence was mostly a non-issue. He did not envisage as an audience the self-preoccupied crowd in the marketplace whom Nietzsche's madman accuses of killing God. However, his paradigm for the purification of awareness is not just about the advanced phases of people's prayer lives, but about the purification of human perception and awareness in general. Ultimately, what he is outlining is the intrinsic link between morality and epistemology, namely, how the accuracy and fullness of all perception depends upon the faith, charity, and hope of the one perceiving. Examining his paradigm, it becomes evident that contemplative wonder, proper perception, passes through the identical stages as Christian prayer and that it depends upon the same conditions for its purification.

Hence his paradigm can serve as a model which can be used to decondition ourselves in general from the distortions of perception caused by our narcissism, pragmatism, and excessive restlessness so as to regain our contemplative faculties. Undergoing the dark night restores to us the fullness of wonder. How?

The dark night of the soul accomplishes within us a triple task in relation to restoring our sense of wonder: i) It gives us the asceticism we need to move beyond the spontaneous dictates of our own narcissism, ii) it breaks narcissism and pragmatism as the motivation for our knowing and loving, and iii) it moves us beyond the congenital propensity we have to relate through conceptual understanding, possessive feelings, and the need for security.

However, to understand how the dark night of the soul accomplishes this triple purification within us, we must first examine how we are triply blocked:

i) Lack of asceticism as blocking wonder

Lack of moral, emotional, and psychological discipline reduces wonder. Why is this? Simply put, because lack of discipline and asceticism invariably lead to increased self-indulgence and self-preoccupation. Without making any moral judgements whatsoever, one can say that self-indulgence and excessive self-preoccupation are the antithesis of genuine awareness. When one is preoccupied with self and the needs of the self, these needs and preoccupations become a mirror through which one then perceives everything else. The other is seen, not as it is in itself, but only as it is in relation to us. Moreover, the other is not only then partially hidden, but is also distorted.

Examples abound: for instance, anyone who does not, and quite vigorously at times, check his feelings of paranoia, self-pity, and resentment will invariably find himself caught up in a depressive self-focus. This depression then has a double effect: first, since depression focuses us upon ourselves, it limits what we notice and are aware of; second, it also causes us to distort what we perceive, that is, we see everything through a set of coloured glasses, in this case, glasses covered with paranoia and suspicion. Moral laxity, similarly, limits and distorts awareness. For example, the person who is sexually indulgent will invariably see others, not as they are in themselves, but as sex objects, as sexual rivals, or as uninteresting because they are not sexually attractive. Always there is an impoverished awareness coupled with projection and distortion.

These examples are simple but they are illustrative. When they are multiplied and extended, as they are in the noncontemplative personality, there is a dramatic narrowing and distortion of awareness.

ii) Pragmatic and narcissistic motivation as blocking wonder

When we approach perception with too many pragmatic and narcissistic concerns our awareness is narrowed accordingly. Reality is not perceived as it is in itself, with all its multifarious dimensions and its riches. It is only perceived as it relates to the categories and containers that our needs and concerns have erected.

A few examples are useful here. Imagine entering a crowded train station in search of a friend. As you search among the crowd of faces for your friend your eyes scan hundreds of faces, but your awareness of these others is superficial and virtually non-existent. You are looking for a particular face and you focus on nothing else. You see hundreds of faces, but your pragmatic concern, however valid in itself, dictates that you perceive only one face, your friend's. This illustrates how our needs and concerns dictate what we actually see and are aware of. Thus, whenever reality is approached with pragmatic concerns, we will notice only certain of its dimensions. However, as this illustration makes clear, there are other dimensions (faces perhaps even more interesting than our friend's) present which are capable of being perceived. Concerns limit awareness. Moreover, as we saw earlier, when those concerns are not just pragmatic, but also selfish, then awareness is not just limited but is distorted as well.

iii) Instinctual reliance upon conceptual knowledge, possessive feelings, and feelings of security as blocking wonder

Every concept, every imaginative construct for understanding, and every feeling through which we possess something in knowledge or love is ultimately inadequate. In the end, these are icons which conceal and limit as much as they reveal. When, in response to our natural instincts, we seek to understand in a conceptual way, when we seek to possess something, and when we seek to control our relationship to things so as to remain secure, then we never fully attain the sheer gaze of admiration, the widest possible agnosticism, and the full gift of wonder.

Again, an example can be helpful. Imagine someone coming up to you and telling you: 'You know, I understand you. I've watched you grow up, I know your Myers-Briggs results, I know your Enneagram number, and I am familiar with the dysfunctions in your family and your background. Besides that, you are French, and I know the temperament of the French! And you are so perfectly your mother's daughter! Oh, yes, I do understand you!' Would you feel very understood? Compare that to someone who comes up to you and says: 'You know, I don't understand you at all! You are one rich mystery! I've known you for twenty years and you still constantly surprise me!' In this latter case, in this non-understanding that admits of wonder and mystery, I suspect, you would feel more understood. The dark night of the spirit which John of the Cross prescribes for the purification of our prayer lives is equally necessary for the purification of our awareness. Unless our normal way of understanding is transformed so that we begin to understand more by not understanding than by understanding we will never truly stand before each other and the world in wonder.

Nikos Kazantzakis once said:

> Truly, nothing more resembles God's eyes than the eyes of a child; they see the world for the first time, and create it. Before this, the world is chaos. All creatures – animals, trees, men, stones, everything: forms, colours, voices, smells, lightning flashes – flow unexplored in front of the child's eyes (no, not in front of them, inside them), and he cannot fasten them down, cannot establish order. The child's world is not made of clay, to last, but of clouds. A cool breeze blows across his temples and the world condenses, attenuates, vanishes. Chaos must have passed in front of God's eyes in just this way before the Creation....[14]

He goes on to say however that, at a point, our senses harden and we begin, precisely, to understand by understanding, and, by that fact, draw ourselves outside the world's embrace, to stand separate: 'As a child sits on his doorstep receiving the world's dense turbid deluge, one day he sees. The five senses have grown firm. Each has carved out its own road and taken its share of the world's kingdom.'[15]

Initially this is immensely freeing and we explode with the pleasure of learning and simply explode with learning. Eventually, though, our senses and what they are connected to harden too much and we lose our wonder and the sense that, as T. S. Eliot once put it, 'the end of all our exploring will be to arrive where we started',[16] that is, in a union beyond concepts. Except that Eliot is not fully correct. We do not arrive at the same spot from where we started. A child is pre-conceptual. Wonder, in the purified awareness of the contemplative, is post-conceptual. A child is in union with things, prior to concepts, while a contemplative is in union with things beyond concepts. The purification of awareness which the mystics describe does not bring us back to the naivete and pre-critical consciousness of a child, it takes us to a post-critical consciousness that is childlike and post-adult. Irrespective of that difference, what this purification of our awareness does is open us again to perceive in a way that has us sitting on the doorstep of reality optimally open to the world's dense turbid deluge, perceiving reality in all its fullness and wildness, face to face.

Kazantzakis adds: 'When I was a child, I became one with sky, insects, sea, wind – whatever I saw or touched ... Shutting my eyes contentedly, I used to hold out my palms and wait. God always came – as long as I remained a child.'[17] The mystical tradition within Christianity assures us of the same thing. God will always come to us ... as long as we, through the painful purification of our awareness that they describe, remain in the perceptive posture of a child.

Notes

1) Nikos Kazantzakis, *Report to Greco*, NY, 1965, pp. 222–223.
2) Matthew 5:8.
3) Anne Frank, *The Diary of a Young Girl*, NY, Doubleday, 1967, p. 134.
4) John of the Cross, *The Dark Night of the Soul*, Book II, chapter 19, no. 1, Kavanaugh, op. cit., p. 373.
5) 1 Corinthians 13:12–13.
6) *Idem*. (My own translation.)
7) For example: *The Dark Night*, Book I, chapter 9, clearly spells out that one will not pass through the *night of the senses* if there is habitual moral laxity ('sin and imperfection'), no regular life of prayer ('weakness and lukewarmness'), and too severe a level of psychological depression ('bad humour or bodily indisposition'). The 'drowning out of God's voice by

constant distraction' is clearly outlined, among other places, in *The Living Flame of Love*, Commentary on Stanza 3, no. 18–23.

8) John of the Cross, *The Ascent of Mount Carmel*, Book I, chapter 13, Kavanaugh, pp. 101–104.

9) John of the Cross, *The Ascent of Mount Carmel*, Book I, chapter 13, no. 11, Kavanaugh, pp. 103–104.

10) Hebrews 11:8.

11) John of the Cross, *The Ascent of Mount Carmel*, Book II, chapter 6, Kavanaugh, pp. 119–121. For a detailed description of the pains, emptiness, and afflictions experienced in the passive night of the spirit, see *The Dark Night*, Book II, chapters 5–8, Kavanaugh, pp. 335–346.

12) John of the Cross, *The Ascent of Mount Carmel*, Book II, chapter 4, Kavanaugh, pp. 112–115.

13) John of the Cross, *The Living Flame of Love*, Commentary on Stanza one, no. 29–32, Kavanaugh, pp. 591–592.

14) Nikos Kazantzakis, *Report to Greco*, pp. 44–45.

In Christian spirituality there is an interesting connection between *seeing* and *sanctity* (a connection not as pronounced in other traditions, even other mystical traditions). In Christianity, *the eyes* are very important. Thus, for example, G. K. Chesterton contrasts how Christian saints are depicted in art as opposed to how Buddhist saints are depicted: 'The opposition exists at every point; but perhaps the shortest statement of it is that the Buddhist saint always has his eyes shut, while the Christian saint always has them wide open. The Buddhist saint has a sleek and harmonious body, but his eyes are heavy and sealed with sleep. The medieval saint's body is wasted to its crazy bones, but his eyes are frightfully alive ... The Buddhist is looking with a peculiar intentness inwards. The Christian is staring with frantic intentness outwards.' (G. K. Chesterton, *Everlasting Man*, NY, 1955, p. 241).

15) *Ibid.*, p. 46.

16) T. S. Eliot, 'Little Gidding', in *Four Quartets*, p. 59.

17) Nikos Kazantzakis, *Report to Greco*, p. 45.

Chapter 5

Contemplation as respecting the holiness of God: the Protestant contemplative tradition

In her book, *Holy the Firm*, Annie Dillard shares with us her quandary regarding picking which church to attend:

> Nothing could more surely convince me of God's unending mercy than the continued existence on earth of the church.
>
> The higher Christian churches – where, if anywhere, I belong – come at God with an unwarranted air of professionalism, with authority and pomp, as though they knew what they were doing, as though people in themselves were an appropriate set of creatures to have dealings without God. I often think of the set pieces of liturgy as certain words which people have successfully addressed to God with their getting killed. In the high churches they saunter through liturgy like Mohawks along a strand of scaffolding who have long since forgotten their danger. If God were to blast such a service to bits, the congregation would be, I believe, genuinely shocked. But in the low churches you expect it any minute. This is the beginning of wisdom.[1]

It is also, in mind of a large segment of Christian thought, the beginning of contemplation.

In the tradition of classical Protestantism, contemplation is understood as a healthy fear of the Lord. We are properly contemplative when we let God be God and live in the face of that holiness.

In caption, that contains the essence of what classical Protestantism considers 'purity of heart' ... we are contemplatives when we live in holy fear of God, namely, when we live by faith rather than by understanding, when we live in humility rather than in boasting, and when we let God give us justification rather than attempting to grasp it all on our own.

Isaiah's reminder that 'God's ways are not our ways';[2] God's reminder to Job that anyone who was not around when the foundations of the universe were being laid should be more into wonder and less into conclusions;[3] and Paul's reminder that we can approach God only through faith and depend, for life, upon his justification rather than upon our own;[4] contain, for Protestantism, the seeds of contemplation. Living those truths is contemplation. This, however, needs much explanation.

Who represents this tradition? Classical Protestantism, in general, embodies this and the very word 'Protestant' implies it. The protest of Luther and the original reformers was not, as is commonly supposed, a protest against Rome and the Roman church. It was, first and foremost, *a protest for God*, a protest against every private and institutional thought or practice which in any way denigrates the absolute holiness and freedom of God and which attempts to approach God more through the categories of human reason rather than those of faith. It is clearly represented in the thought of Luther and Calvin. More recently it is less clearly manifest along denominational lines, and so can be seen in Protestant, Anglican, and Roman Catholic circles alike. In Protestantism it is seen, most clearly, in the thought of Karl Barth and his Neo-Orthodox followers and, with a slightly different nuance, in Jurgen Moltmann. Among Roman Catholic and Anglican/Episcopalian thinkers it is manifest in such persons as Hans Urs Von Balthasar, Gustavo Gutierrez, and Alan Jones.

Among all these thinkers, past and present, there is present the idea that the experience of the death of God is, in the end, due to a breakdown in contemplation ... and, for them, *to contemplate is to live always in a holy fear of God*.

NON-CONTEMPLATIVENESS AS THE LOSS OF THE SENSE OF GOD'S HOLINESS

G. K. Chesterton once commented that our perennial spiritual and psychological task is *to learn to look at things familiar until they become unfamiliar again.*[5] The Protestant contemplative tradition would agree and would insist that this is nowhere more imperative than in our relationship with God, the Holy One.

God, as scripture and church teachings assure us, is holy. Holiness, however, must be properly understood. It does not connote piety, as is the common assumption. Holiness, biblically, means *otherness, incomprehensibility, beyond conception, beyond imagination, awesome, awe-ful.* As holy, God is antithetical to finite creatures. The infinite is not like the finite.[6] Hence, when Isaiah has his vision of God in the temple and is left gasping and simply repeating the words, 'Holy, Holy, Holy, is the Lord God of hosts'[7] his words might best be paraphrased: 'Other, awesome, completely beyond what we can see, think, feel, imagine, or capture in words is the Lord God of hosts!' Isaiah then goes on to say that our response to that holiness must be a holy fear, an acceptance of the fact that in our understanding we can never capture God or understand the ways of God.

This concept of God's otherness and our need to respect it, is central to the teachings of the New Testament. Not only do we see it as the pivotal theme in Paul's letters, especially to the Romans and Galatians, but Jesus makes a virtual pedagogy out of it in his revelation of God. In the parables, for example, we see a constant iconoclasm, a constant subverting and smashing of people's familiar notions of God in such a way that out of the ruins comes an invitation to a new understanding of God. In Jesus' entire revelation, but especially in the parables, we see the challenge to let God be God.

Looking at Jesus' parables, for instance, we see that although the stories are about people, the real plot is God. They are revelatory, revealing the heart of God. Moreover what they do reveal is that the heart of God, the divine mystery, cannot be pinned down or definitively psyched out by human projections and expectations. It is always most dangerous to presuppose that God must feel and think as we do! The parables try to move us beyond that temptation. They reveal a God whose heart is full of surprises and who has perspectives far beyond our expectations. We see this, for instance, with unequivocal clarity in the parable of the prodigal son[8] (none of Christ's listeners could have guessed the Father's reaction), in the parable of the vineyard workers[9] (who would have guessed that the last workers would receive the same pay as the first ones?) and in the parable of the good Samaritan[10] (who would have guessed that the priest would pass by and the enemy, the Samaritan, would stop?)

In the parables, and in Christ's revelation in general, there is always an element of astonishment, surprise, the unexpected. The logic and measured expectation of those hearing revelation is always shattered. The three parables just cited illustrate this well. In each of them there is present the element of surprise, Jesus' listeners would have been astonished and the astonishment and surprise were the result of realising that God is infinitely other and infinitely more than they had anticipated. In John Shea's words, God was always *more* than they had anticipated:

For as Mark says,
'He was too much for them'.
Like a woman who loves too much
like ointment that costs too much
and is spilled too much
like a seventy times seven God
who forgives too much
like a seed that grows too much
and yields thirty
    sixty
    a hundred fold.[11]

Christ's revelation of God then is iconoclastic and subversive in that it constantly smashes our preconceptions, unexamined ideas, biases, narrowness, projections, and logical expectations and nowhere does it do that more than in regard to our concept of God. In short, Jesus shatters the image of God that logical expectation builds up and, from its ruins, invites us to live in a new wonder. Jesus assures us that the heart of the infinite cannot be pinned down, captured, or psyched out through human understanding. Prescriptively, Christ says: 'Do not try to capture God. Live in wonder. Let your agnosticism be very very wide. Do not try to understand the infinite within the confines of finite experience.'

Invariably, however, that is precisely what we attempt to do and we do it in two interrelated, yet distinct, ways: 1) At the level of our thought and theologising, we approach God through the categories of human understanding rather than through the categories of faith. We make God meet human expectations, whether these be metaphysical, psychological, or moral. 2) At the level of our actual living, we attempt to be our own justification rather then letting God give us righteousness. In either case, the purity of heart needed for contemplation breaks down and God eventually dies within our experience.

Let us examine this in some detail:

1) *Approaching God through the categories of human understanding – Job's friends*

Christian revelation is clear, God is holy. God's ways are not our ways: God is wholly other and, thus, inaccessible to human understanding; the infinite cannot and may not be understood within finite categories. To live in a proper fear of God demands acknowledging and living in the face of this.

In ways subtle and not-so-subtle, and in ways theoretical and not-so-theoretical, we constantly infringe upon these truths. Rarely, in the way we think or the way we live, are we able to respect fully the holiness of God. More commonly we give in to our propensity to make the infinite God fit into the finite limits of our human minds and hearts. When we do this, then, like Job's friends, we create a God who is, in the end, no bigger than our own imaginations. Moreover, we run the risk of ending up in a negative agnosticism or atheism because any God who is not the full awesome holy God of revelation will eventually not be worth our belief and worship.

Put more simply, the Protestant contemplative tradition understands contemplation as follows: the God of Judeo-Christian and Islamic revelation (not to mention the God of Hinduism, Buddhism, and Taoism) is a God who is infinite and, therefore, beyond the possibility of being grasped by the finite human mind, heart, or imagination. Such a God is, by definition, *non-conceptualisable and non-imaginable*. So, too, are the ways of that God. That is what is meant when we say that God is holy. Given this, a proper relationship to God can only be one of backing off and giving God the space within which to be God. Unlike Job's friends, we must avoid psychological univocity, that is, the idea that God must think, feel, act, and be as we are. To fall into this, however subtle a form it might take, is to make God less than God and to fall out of contemplation. Let me attempt to illustrate this with an example.

Several years ago, Harold Kushner released a book entitled *When Bad Things Happen to Good People*[12] which immediately became a best-seller. It is a deeply compassionate reflection upon human suffering and how God might be conceived of in the light of suffering. Essentially, Kushner's thesis runs as follows. How can God be all-loving and all-powerful in the light of the fact that there is so much random and seemingly senseless suffering on earth? Young children die of cancer. Young mothers whose children desperately need them are struck down through accidents, illness, and other random circumstances. There is so much unnecessary and inexplicable suffering. How can an all-powerful God permit this?

Kushner's question is not new. It is the perennial question of evil and suffering. What is more novel, both within the tradition of Judaism (from which he comes) and Christianity, is his answer. Kushner concludes that God is *not* all-powerful and all-loving. God is all-loving; but, in unredeemed suffering, we see that God is not all-powerful. In Kushner's thesis, if God had the radical power to stop random suffering he would stop it and, since he does not stop it, we can conclude that God is not all-powerful.

What is clear is that Kushner's thought is more in line with that of Job's friends than with that of Job. Despite his deep compassion, this book is, in the end, an example, and a very good one at that, of psychological univocity. Bottom-line, what is being said is that since *we* cannot make sense of something then *that something cannot make sense at all*, there is no perspective beyond our own, no higher perspective within which what we cannot now understand might be understood. Whatever else this conception is, ultimately, it is a slimming down of God to fit the size, expectations, and reasoning of the human mind and imagination. The infinite is being understood by the finite. Perhaps, as some argue, this serves to make God more accessible to us and allows us more easily to understand God's compassion. Be that as it may, it has, according to the Protestant tradition of contemplation, a potentially lethal dysfunction, namely, a God who is not allowed to be God beyond our human understanding and imagination will in due time be rejected for precisely those reasons, for being less than God!

Several years ago, a famous Canadian journalist, Gordon Sinclair, died. For many years he had been a regular panellist on a nationally televised news programme. An avowed atheist, Sinclair had for years given the Canadian public his apologia for atheism. It ran as follows. As a young journalist he had gone to India to cover the wars surrounding India's struggles with Britain. While there he saw human misery and death at such a magnitude that his mind and heart could simply not reconcile this with the existence of God. In his words, 'God is simply not imaginable in the face of that kind of suffering and meaninglessness.'

Had he presented this apologia to Isaiah, Job, Luther, or Calvin he would have received a surprising answer. They would have said simply: 'You're right! In the face of that kind of suffering, one cannot *imagine* that God exists! But the issue here is precisely one of imagining! Belief in God and faith in God is not had on the basis of being able to *imagine* the existence of such a presence. In fact, when you try to imagine God, if you at all look very hard at certain issues, you will end up in atheism!' Why? Because all attempts to picture God imaginatively and to rationally *understand* how the existence of such a Being can be consistent with everything we see is an enterprise that, by definition, undercuts our ability to believe in God. A few illustrations will make this clear.

Thus, for example, looking at the world from the perspective of its unwholeness, at the perennial presence of suffering and evil, one could argue, as many do, that either God cannot exist, exists but is not all-powerful, or is himself malicious, quixotic, and incompetent. Our world is all too full of evil, physical and moral. We can speak of physical evil in the many destructive and death-producing phenomena within nature – infectious parasites, cancer, the AIDS virus, natural disasters, among other things. These inflict death, pain, disease, and destruction randomly and senselessly. More serious still is the presence of moral evil: cruelty (even among children), selfishness, exploitation, rape, murder, insensitivity and stupidity of multiple sorts, man being a wolf to man![13] With evil being so widespread, how can we conceive of a benevolent, all-powerful creator who is lovingly coaxing creation to higher and more loving levels of existence? How can the existence of an all-powerful and all-loving God be conceived of and imagined in the face of this evidence?

Perhaps even more challenging is the task of trying to conceive of and imagine the existence of God in the face of the overwhelming immensity of our universe and the infinite multiplicity of phenomena within it. When one goes out at night and looks at the stars, the light of those that are closest to us, travelling at the unimaginable speed of 186,000 miles per second, has taken four years to get here. The light from those that are most distant from us, travelling at that same unimaginable speed, has taken 800,000 years to reach us ... and scientists have seen stars through x-ray telescopes whose light has not yet reached the earth, which are 6 trillion light years from our earth. The immensity of our universe simply stuns the imagination. These distances simply cannot be imaginatively conceived. Given this, and given that there are perhaps hundreds of billions of galaxies with trillions of light years separating them, and given that on each of the planets within each of those galaxies there are hundreds of trillions of phenomena happening every second (and this through billions of years), can we really believe that somewhere there is a person, a heart, so supreme and all-knowing that it created all of this; and that, right now, it knows minutely and intimately every detail and happening and that it is passionately concerned with every one of those happenings?

To expatiate further with just one small example. Our planet, earth, is just one of many billions of planets. Yet, just on it, during each second of time there are hundreds of persons being born, hundreds of persons are being conceived, hundreds of others are dying, millions are sinning, millions are doing virtuous acts, millions are suffering, millions are celebrating, millions are hoping, millions are praying, many are despairing, and all of this has been happening for hundreds of thousands of years. Can we really believe that a God exists who intimately knows all of this in every detail, cares passionately about each individual detail, and is, somehow, Lord over all of this so that 'no sparrow falls from the sky or no hair from a human head' without that Lord knowing and caring deeply? Can we *imagine* the existence of God in the face of all this?

The answer quite simply is *no*! When one considers the presence of evil and the sheer immensity and multiplicity of phenomena, among other things, one cannot imagine or conceive of a God who could truly be lord and master of all of this. Our minds and imaginations simply cannot stretch far enough to conceive of that. We simply cannot *picture* it. But that is the precise point at issue, the divine reality cannot be grasped through a finite imagination. The limits of human imagination and its frustrations and breakdown *vis-à-vis* imagining the existence or presence of God are not to be identified with the possibility of the existence or non-existence of God. The fact that we cannot imagine that God exists speaks more about the finitude of the mind and the incredibly holy character of the infinite than it does about the likelihood or unlikelihood of the existence of such an infinite being.

Many difficulties in believing in God's existence, not even to mention difficulties in prayer, arise from our failure to recognise and appropriate this. Thus, for example, suppose, one night, I lie in bed, stare holes into the darkness, try to imagine the existence of God, and come up dry ... I try to picture and feel God's existence, but cannot and I begin to panic: 'Dear God, I am an atheist! I can no longer imagine and feel that God exists! God doesn't exist!' Then, on another night, I lie in bed and I feel very secure in my sense that God exists and I can imagine that existence. Does this mean that on the one night I have faith in God and on the other I do not? No. More accurately, one night I have a strong imagination and on the other night I do not! The difference lies not in God's existence or non-existence, but largely in the capacity or incapacity of the imagination to crank up its own constructs which either give one the sense that God exists or leave one unable imaginatively to picture and feel this.

Frustrations in attempting to conceive of and imaginatively picture and feel God and God's relationship to creation tend to lead, as they did in Gordon Sinclair's case, to the unfounded conclusion that, because we cannot think, picture or imaginatively understand how it is possible, God does not exist. This, however, is precisely *psychological univocity*, the failure to accept properly the holiness of God. Like Job's friends, we are saying that if the best human minds cannot make sense of it, then it cannot make sense at all!

Ultimately, the Protestant tradition would say, this is a breakdown in contemplation. The atheism that arises from our incapacity to conceive of God is, in the end, an idolatry that results from not properly respecting God's holiness. God has been slimmed down to fit within the limits of a finite heart and mind. Such a God is then, precisely, unable to measure up intellectually because (and this is a strange paradox) an intellectually conceivable God is, ultimately, inconceivable intellectually. A God that can be understood will, at a point, become non-understandable! As the examples given above demonstrate, it is only possible to conceive of God when we let God's way be above our ways!

But where does that leave us? If God cannot be conceived of, what alternatives remain? How can we know God? Are we doomed to either agnosticism or to blind faith based solely on authority and revelation?

For the Protestant contemplative tradition there is another option: awe and wonder! God can be approached through these. God cannot be understood in concepts and the existence of God cannot be captured imaginatively or even felt in a possessive feeling, but he can be experienced, touched, and undergone. God cannot be *thought*, but God can be *met*. Through awe and wonder we *experience* God and there, as the mystics have always stated, we understand more by not understanding than by understanding. In that posture we let God be God. In such a posture, too, we live in contemplation.

All of this, however, takes place mostly at the level of thought. How do we, in the view of Protestantism, denigrate the holiness of God at the level of *praxis*? How do we, in our day to day lives, not let God be God?

2) *Our attempts at self-justification block the justification that only God can give us – human boasting*

To let God be God implies not only that we do not, by our intellectual and imaginative constructs, set limits to the infinite, but also, and especially, that we allow God to give us meaning, significance, uniqueness, and eternal life rather than trying to grasp these for ourselves. To be a contemplative means that we must not 'boast' but must be 'saved by faith alone'.[14] What does this mean?

Alan Jones, who healthily straddles a number of contemplative traditions, including this one, sums this up succinctly:

> We nurse within our hearts the hope that we are different, that we are special, that we are extraordinary. We long for the assurance that our birth was no accident, that a god had a hand in our coming to be, that we exist by divine fiat. We ache for a cure for the ultimate disease of mortality. Our madness comes when the pressure is too great and we fabricate a vital lie to cover up the fact that we are mediocre, accidental, mortal. We fail to see the glory of the Good News. The vital lie is unnecessary because all the things we long for have been given us freely.[15]

One of our great temptations in life is this vital lie, which amounts to what scripture calls 'boasting' and 'self-righteousness'. As Jones points out, we are born with the innate knowledge, wired to the fact that we are unique, significant, precious, and destined for eternal life. But this intuition, however deeply felt, tends to wilt under the pressure of trying to live a life that is unique and special in a world in which billions of others are trying to do the same thing. Can billions be infinitely precious and utterly unique?

Inevitably the fear of anonymity and mortality overwhelms us. When we feel this, and outside of a deep faith it can be the dominant feeling during the second half of our lives, we begin to believe that we are precious, meaningful, and unique *only* when we accomplish something which precisely sets us apart and ensures that we are unique and will be remembered.

For most of us, the dominant obsession of adult life is that of trying to guarantee our own preciousness, loveableness, meaning, immortality, and sanctity. In the end, we do not believe we can have these independent of our own accomplishments and so we fabricate the lie, we try to make a mark for ourselves, rather than letting God give us this.

In the tradition of Protestantism, contemplation means to back off and let God be God. This implies, as we saw, that we do not, like Job's friends, limit God by psyching him out, but it also means that we do not attempt to be justified by anything and anybody other than God alone. *Faith alone saves!* That simple line contains the Protestant prescriptive counsel for contemplation: Let God give you preciousness, meaning, significance, and eternal life. Do not try to guarantee these for yourself.

To let God be holy, and to let God's ways be above our ways, means that we must also trust God to give us preciousness, meaning, and eternal life *beyond* our ways.

When Nietzsche's madman turned on the crowd in the marketplace and accused them of being God's murderers, Isaiah, Job, and Paul would have secretly smiled. For they would have understood why, for the most part, God was dead and how he had been killed. In the consciousness of the marketplace, with all its heartaches, headaches, and restlessness there is very little wonder and awe, very little backing off so that God can be God. Whenever that happens, God cannot reveal and God cannot give us meaning and significance because there is no space within which to do it. God dies within human life when there is no space within which God can be holy.

CONTEMPLATION AS FAITH, FEAR OF THE LORD, WONDER, AND RELIANCE ON JUSTIFICATION BY GOD

The cross is the utterly incommensurable factor in the revelation of God. We have become far too used to it. We have surrounded the scandal of the cross with roses. We have made a theory of salvation out of it. But that is not the cross. That is not the blackness inherent in it, placed in it by God. Hegel defined the cross: 'God is dead' – and he no doubt rightly saw that here we are faced with the night of the real, ultimate and inexplicable absence of God, and that before the 'Word of the cross' we are dependent upon the principle SOLA FIDE; dependent upon it as nowhere else. Here we have not the OPERA DEI, which point to him as the eternal creator, and to his wisdom. Here the faith in creation, the source of all paganism, breaks down. Here this whole philosophy and wisdom is abandoned to folly. Here God is non-God. Here is the triumph of death, the enemy, the non-church, the lawless state, the blasphemer, the soldiers. Here Satan triumphs over God. *Our faith begins at the point where atheists suppose that it must be at an end. Our faith begins with the bleakness and power which is the night of the cross, abandonment, temptation, and doubt about everything that exists!*

Our faith must be born where it is abandoned by all tangible reality; it must be born of nothingness, it must taste this nothingness and be given it to taste in a way no philosophy of nihilism can imagine.[16]

With that quote, Jurgen Moltmann captures the essence of the Protestant contemplative tradition, that is, faith begins where atheism thinks it ends and it is born where it is abandoned by all tangible reality, including the thoughts of our intellects and the spontaneous feelings of our hearts.

Contemplation, long before this designates any explicit prayer activity or prayer technique, means to live in such a way that God can enter into our lives. What is emphasised in the Protestant tradition is that we must live in such a way and think in such a way that we do not put any limits on God and upon our capacity to be open to God. This has various levels.

Metaphysically this means accepting what the Fourth Lateran Council (1215) taught, namely, that the difference between God and creature is infinitely greater than any similarity.[17] Consequently we may not conclude that bad things happening to good people implies God is not all-powerful. The metaphysical and religious speculations of Job's friends block true contemplation. We do too, when we join them!

Psychologically and intellectually this means we must respect the fact that all concepts and imaginative constructs that we form of God and of God's ways are fundamentally inadequate to understand God.

Emotionally this means that we must learn to live with the insecurity of an understanding of God which understands more by not understanding. We must be able to live with mystery, unsolved riddles, and unrequited emotional suffering.

In brief, to contemplate we must learn to live in, what mystics have always described as, a certain darkness, emotional as well as intellectual. God can reveal to us only when with our heads, our emotions, and our actions, we do not block that revelation.

Metaphorically, this idea might be captured in Elizabeth Barrett Browning's one-line exegesis on God's invitation to Moses as he approaches the burning bush. God told Moses: 'Take off your shoes because the ground you are standing on is holy ground!'[18] Browning paraphrases God's invitation into a universal prescription for contemplation: 'The earth is ablaze with the fire of God, but only those who see it take their shoes off. The rest sit around and pick blackberries!'[19]

That, according to the Protestant tradition of contemplation, is what it means to let God be God. In that view, when Nietzsche's madman accuses the crowd in the busy marketplace of being God's murderers he is, exactly, catching them with their shoes on, picking blackberries!

More specifically, however, how does all of this translate into a contemplative *praxis*? How do we, in the practical task of living, let God be God?

An outline for contemplation within the Protestant tradition might be captured within four prescriptive counsels: 1) Approach God through faith, not understanding; 2) Undergo God's presence rather than trying to figure out that presence; 3) Live in holy fear of God; and 4) Let God be your justification rather than trying to guarantee your own. We will examine each briefly.

1) *Approach God through faith, not understanding*
Understanding takes place on the basis of intellectual and imaginative constructs. Faith takes place on the basis of trust. Our natural propensity is to demand understanding and to be most uncomfortable and impatient whenever it is not there. This

proclivity to need *to make sense* of everything rather than to live in a trust that goes beyond this, is a God-given instinct and is both good and necessary for us to live as human beings. It serves us well, in most realms. However, at a certain point, it does not serve us *vis-à-vis* our relationship to God. As we saw earlier with the mystical tradition, it is a metaphysics that we must ultimately transcend so as to live in faith.

What is at stake here, the difference between understanding and faith, becomes clearer when we look at some examples. Henri Nouwen gives a gripping example of this from his own life; how he, himself, had to move from understanding to faith.

In his book, *In Memoriam*, he describes the death of his mother. He begins his account with his own feelings as he is flying home from New York to Amsterdam to be at her side as she is dying. Since his mother had been a wonderful, generous, very Christian, very loving, and very gracious woman, he felt that her death would radiate precisely those qualities. As he is flying home on the plane, he thinks in gratitude of her and imagines a scenario in which her death will be a capstone on such a gracious and Christian life.

The reality that confronts him at her bedside shatters his naive expectations. His mother lies dying, not in the calm of peace, as one might expect in the case of someone who had lived so generous and good a life, but in the grip of struggle, pain, even terror. Confronted by this, Nouwen asks the perennially poignant questions: Why? How can this make sense? If there is a God, how can all this be happening? His answer? We do not understand. We cannot understand. Our minds, imaginations, and hearts are too finite, too limited. We cannot see the whole picture, the gap between the infinite and the finite cannot be bridged by understanding but only by faith and wonder:

Why, why were we witnessing such pain and agony in a woman whose life had been one of goodness, gentleness, tenderness and love...?

During the days of mother's dying, I heard that question repeated frequently. Often, friends suggested that it was unfair for this lovely woman to suffer such a painful death. Many were adamant that she did not deserve such a wrenching struggle. But do we really understand?

103

Slowly, as the long hours and days passed, I began to wonder if mother's struggle did not in fact reveal the awesome truth of God's love. Who was more loving than Jesus? Who suffered more than he? Jesus' life of faithful service did not end in a peaceful, tranquil death. He who was without sin suffered an agony of immeasurable depth; his cry of the cross, 'God, O God, why have you forsaken me?' still echoes down through the centuries.

Is it this agony that mother was called to share? Is it this cross that she was invited to feel more deeply than others? I do not know. I cannot say yes or no to these questions. What really took place during the hours of her death cannot be explained or made understandable. But the thought that she who had loved so many, given so much and felt so deeply, was called to be united with Christ even in his agony, did not leave me during these days.

Friends kept saying to me, 'Your mother always thought of others first.' That is true. She lived for others, for her husband, her children, her grandchildren, her friends. She indeed had the mind of Christ, always considering the other person to be better than herself. But that does not necessarily lead to a smooth death. Why do we think that the hope for a life with Christ will make our death like a gentle passage? A compassionate life is a life in which the suffering of others is deeply felt, and such a life may also make one's death an act of dying with others. When I saw mother's battle, her cry of hope and faith, I wondered if she was not crying with the many others for whom she had lived.

In Jesus' agony we see the agony of the world in all its gripping intensity: Sadness came over him, and great distress. Then he said ... 'My soul is sorrowful to the point of death.' (Matthew 26:37). Is not every human being who wants to live with the mind of Christ also called to die with the mind of Christ? ...

What then is this agony? Is it fear of God, fear of punishment, fear of the immensity of the divine presence? I do not know, but if I have any sense of what I saw, it was more profound. It was the fear of the great abyss which separates God from us, a distance which can only be bridged by faith.[20]

What Nouwen shows in this description is the movement from understanding to faith, from a reliance upon imaginative constructs and possessive feelings to trust. This is the essence of contemplation. When the wells of logical expectations, feeling, imagination, and intellectual understanding run dry, when obfuscation threatens to turn to despair, and when it seems impossible imaginatively to feel God's existence and goodness in the face of some concrete fact, but we continue to live in an openness which refuses to set limits, then we are contemplating. It is also then, and only then, that we have our shoes off before the burning bush, that we are living in wonder, and are letting God be God.

One qualifier should be added here however: in affirming that faith is not understanding, this tradition does not affirm that faith *goes against* understanding or that faith is based upon blind trust. Faith, while taking us *beyond* understanding does not denigrate understanding any more than Einstein's physics denigrates grade-school arithmetic, reality denigrates a photograph, or the light of dawn denigrates a candle burning in the night. It just goes infinitely beyond. And what was grasped in the mind and heart before faith's light eclipsed it was real and it remains in such a way that the trust in which we now live takes its root in there. Grade-school arithmetic does not disappear when Einstein appears, a photograph of someone does not become unreal when you actually see that person, and a candle still gives off light even when a bright sun eclipses that light; they remain as the foundation through which we move on to trust in that which is greater than they are.

2) *Undergo God's presence rather than trying to figure out that presence*

Within the Protestant contemplative tradition the presence of God is not something to be studied, analysed, conceptualised, figured out, or captured. As John Shea so aptly puts it: 'God is not a law to be obeyed but a presence to be seized and acted on.'[21] What does this mean?

In an analogy which comes from Jesus – 'Take the fig tree as a parable; as soon as its twigs grow supple and its leaves come out, you know that summer is near'[22] – we see that to let God be God means to undergo the presence of God as a tree undergoes the presence of summer. The metaphor is extraordinarily simple: a tree is brought to bloom by summer. It does not capture summer, understand summer, conceptualise summer, nor is it even able to project what summer will do to it. It simply *undergoes* summer, acts under its presence. To let God be God is to live in an openness to the mystery and presence of God without limiting the nature or effect of that mystery and presence by any pre-set expectations or by any premature withdrawal from it. In short, the task of contemplation is not that of trying to figure out God or to specify what conditions must be met before we believe in God's existence, power, or goodness. Rather the task of contemplation is, through a dark contemplation analogous to a tree undergoing summer, to simply let God be God. The proper approach to God is not to try to capture the presence of the infinite, but rather to celebrate that presence.

When we do this we end up in a contemplative wonder within which we do not try to conceptualise, imaginatively picture, or possessively feel the nature of God. Then, in the face of all the hard agnostic and bitter questions concerning evil, suffering, and God's seeming absence and impotence, we will be drawn into the posture of the mature Job who achieved a profound understanding by not understanding. When he finally let God be God, he exclaimed:

> I know that you are all-powerful;
> what you conceive, you can perform.
> I am the man who has obscured your designs
> with my empty-headed words.
> I have been holding forth on matters I cannot understand,
> on marvels beyond me and my knowledge ...
> My words have been frivolous: What can I reply?
> I had better lay my finger on my lips.

I have spoken once ... I will not speak again;
More than once ... I will add nothing.[23]

3) *Live in holy fear of God*

Fear of the Lord is the beginning of wisdom. It is also, within the tradition of Protestantism, the beginning of contemplation. Contemplation means, precisely, living in a holy fear of God. What is meant by that? Before attempting to explicate what a healthy fear of God is, it is useful to state what is unhealthy fear.

When the Protestant tradition highlights scripture's dictum that the fear of the Lord is the beginning of wisdom it is not referring to the many pejorative connotations that this expression most often brings to mind, namely, fear that God will punish us if we do not do good; submission to God out of timidity, lack of courage, or lack of nerve; lack of creativity in our lives because we fear, however inchoately, that our own achievements somehow threaten God (like the myth of Prometheus); or a fear of truly enjoying our lives because every time we do we feel that somehow we are stealing pleasure from God. All of these are unhealthy fears, are psychologically rooted, and are antithetical to a truly holy fear of God.

Healthy fear of God is constituted by four interpenetrating elements: i) Living in respect, wonder, and awe; ii) Backing off and not limiting God through our own preconceptions and demands; iii) a lived appropriation of the fact that God is Lord; and iv) a true sense of humility.

We examine each of these briefly:

i) *Living in respect, wonder, and awe*

G. K. Chesterton once suggested that 'the greatest of all illusions is the illusion of familiarity.'[24] Familiarity is also the death of respect, wonder, and awe. When our minds, hearts, and imaginations are no longer poised for surprise and astonishment, when we feel that we have already understood something, then we no longer have a healthy fear of God or indeed of each other. A healthy fear of God means living in such a way that nothing becomes too familiar to us.

We can understand this more clearly if we look at where holy fear breaks down in our interpersonal relations. When we examine our deepest resentments we find that invariably,

107

at their roots, lies the fact that someone has not respected us. How have they not respected us? Usually the violation, on the surface, is not blatant. Almost always it is subtle: they have taken us for granted; they have assumed that they have understood us and our motives, boxed us in with their own preconceived notions; not respected our uniqueness, mystery, and complexity; and taken as owed to them what we can only offer as gift. That is the illusion of familiarity and it is that which is expressed in the axiom: *familiarity breeds contempt.*

To live in fear of God therefore implies, precisely, that we live before God and the rest of reality in such a way that there is never contempt within us. We take nothing for granted, everything as gift. This is respect and it implies that we do not live as if we have already understood. To live in respect is to live in wonder, in a healthy agnosticism, poised always for surprise before the mystery of God, others, and ourselves. To live in a holy fear of God means letting everyone's reality be as huge, mysterious, dark, and complex as it actually is. All boredom and contempt is an infallible sign that we have fallen out of a healthy fear of God.

ii) Backing off and not limiting God through our own pre-conceptions and demands

To fear God is to give God the space within which to be God, beyond our wildest imaginings of what a God should be. We lose proper fear of God when we do not, as Michael Buckley puts it, let God 'contradict the programs and expectations of human beings in order to fulfil human desires and human freedom at a much deeper level than subjectivity would have measured out in its projections.'[25] To fear God means to set aside our own expectations, needs, and imaginings and let God set the agenda and God define the limits. Our posture must be that of the mature Job ... a finger over our mouth![26]

iii) A lived appropriation of the fact that God is Lord

A healthy fear of God brings with it a sense which must flow over into our actions that our freedom is not unconditional but conscienced. When we fear God, we fear misusing our freedom, not because we fear God will punish us if we do wrong, but because we fear hurting others, fear idolatry, and fear self-inflation.

To live in holy fear of God means to bring one's freedom under the Lordship of God. This will be analysed more fully in the next chapter. Suffice it here to say that one lives in holy fear of God when she or he is aware that freedom is a gift given us *for* love and that, outside its continual genuflection before a God beyond itself, it very quickly usurps that role, becomes a god unto itself, and leaves in its wake a trail of violation, idolatry, and self-inflation. In a healthy fear of God, one realises the truth of Karl Rahner's words: 'How often I have found out that we grow to maturity not by doing what we like, but by doing what we should. How true it is that not every *should* is a compulsion, and not every *like* is a high morality and true freedom.'[27]

iv) A true sense of humility
One has a healthy fear of God when one lives in genuine humility. What does this mean?

Before going on to suggest positively what it means to be *humble* it is useful to dissociate that idea from some of its more common misconceptions. To live in humility should not be confused with timidity, shyness, introversion, or a bad self-image. It is not necessarily the self-deprecating person who constantly protests that he or she cannot do the job or should not be asked to lead who is the most humble. That kind of self-depreciation and hesitation can be more the product of a bad self-image, or a natural introversion and timidity, than the product of healthy humility.

The word humility comes from the Latin root *humus* which means soil or earth. Its primary connotation comes from that. To be humble is to be earthy, connected to the soil. The implications of that are triple: i) To be connected to the earth is precisely not to be disconnected and to have your head in the clouds. ii) To be earthy is also to feel your dependence and interconnectedness with others and with the earth. Finally, iii) to be earthy means to keep your shoes off before the burning bush in that the earthy person is in touch with the earth and, figuratively, does not have the skins of dead animals, rubbers, or plastics (what shoes are made of) between herself and the earth.

To be humble therefore is to have a felt sense of your *earthiness and creatureliness*, that is, of your limits, your dependence, your interdependence, your vulnerability, and your connectedness to the soil. The humblest person you know is not the person who lives a timid life but the person who lives a life that constantly acknowledges its limits, its vulnerability, its interconnectedness, and its radical incarnate character.

In our humility we recognise that we are a child of the earth, dust; that we are radically dependent upon the earth and interdependent with each other; and that we must fear always losing our awareness of those connections. This is a holy fear, one which we owe to God, to each other, to the earth, and to ourselves.

In the Protestant tradition this holy fear of God lies at the very heart of contemplation. When it dies, God dies within human experience.

3) *Let God be your justification rather than trying to guarantee your own*

At the deepest root, each of us aches for significance, meaning, uniqueness, preciousness, immortality, and to have in our lives a great love and great beauty. This ache is congenital, incurable, obsessive. We are, as Plato said, fired into life with this divine restlessness in us. However, as Alan Jones says, our madness comes, as we saw, when the pressure gets too great and we ache for a cure for our mortality and insignificance and so we fabricate the vital lie.[28] We try through our own efforts, to create for ourselves significance, uniqueness, and immortality.

In the Protestant tradition, contemplation is the antithesis of this. We contemplate, we put our hearts, minds, and lives in the correct posture, when we resist our spontaneous inclinations to achieve these things for ourselves and, instead, let God give them to us. It is precisely when we are obsessed with and driven by goals which serve to establish and ensure our uniqueness, preciousness, and immortality that we fall into the unhealthy narcissism, pragmatism, and excessive restlessness that constitutes the consciousness of the marketplace within which Nietzsche's madman smashed his lantern and declared that God is dead. When we are driven by goals which would fabricate for us the vital lie, we degenerate into a greed in spirit and in body which makes wonder, awe, full awareness, and the sheer gaze of admiration impossible. When we are trying to guarantee our own significance the posture of our minds, hearts, and lives

110

is not one of contemplation, but one of possessive clutching.

In her insightful diaries, Etty Hillesum captures what is at stake here in an insight that is rare in both its directness and clarity. Commenting upon her own painful struggle to let go of trying to fabricate the vital lie, Hillesum writes:

And here I have hit upon something essential. Whenever I saw a beautiful flower, what I longed to do with it was press it to my heart, or eat it all up. It was more difficult with a piece of beautiful scenery, but the feeling was the same. I was too sensual, I might almost write too greedy. I yearned physically for all I thought was beautiful, wanted to own it. Hence that painful longing that could never be satisfied, the pining for something I thought unattainable, which I called my creative urge. I believe it was this powerful emotion that made me think that I was born to produce great works. It all suddenly changed, God alone knows by what inner process, but it is different now. I realised it only this morning, when I recalled my short walk round the Skating Club a few nights ago. It was dusk, soft hues in the sky, mysterious silhouettes of houses, trees alive with the light through the tracery of their branches, in short, enchanting. And then I knew precisely how I had felt in the past. Then all the beauty would have gone like a stab to my heart and I would not have known what to do with the pain. Then I would have felt the need to write, to compose verses, but the words would still have refused to come. I would have felt utterly miserable, wallowed in the pain and exhausted myself as a result. The experience would have sapped all my energy. Now I know it for what it was: mental masturbation.

But that night, only just gone, I reacted quite differently. I felt that God's world was beautiful despite everything, but its beauty now filled me with joy. I was just as deeply moved by that mysterious, still landscape in the dusk as I might have been before, but somehow I no longer wanted to own it. I went home invigorated and got to work. And the scenery stayed with me, in the background, as a cloak about my soul, to put it

111

poetically for once, but it no longer held me back: I no longer 'masturbated' with it.[29]

What Hillesum is describing here is, precisely, contemplation. As long as she was attempting to press the flower to her heart and to *own* beauty the result was obsessive pain, constant restlessness, a deep narcissism, and no sense of God. Conversely, once she stopped trying to take beauty to herself in such a way so as to assure her own beauty, uniqueness, preciousness, and meaning, she was able to relate to it with the sheer gaze of admiration.

The sheer gaze of admiration is contemplation. It is the gaze which undercuts narcissism, obsessive pragmatism, and excessive restlessness. It is also that gaze which undercuts the consciousness of marketplace which, in Nietzsche's words, murders God. The Protestant obsession with the fact that we may never attempt to give ourselves justification underscores, among other things, that point.

LETTING GOD BE GOD

Immediately after God told Moses to take off his shoes before the burning bush, Moses asked God: 'What is your name?' God answered: '*Yahweh ... I am who am.*'[30] This name does not imply, as medieval commentators suggested, that God is saying 'I am the Being of Beings, the Ground of Being, or the one who causes everything that is.' What it does imply is something much less metaphysical, more personal, and directly significant for what it means to live contemplatively. *I am who am* does not refer to God as the cause or ground of being, but refers to God's freedom, transcendence, and holiness. Paraphrased, God's answer to Moses might read: 'I am the one who cannot be captured in thought, imagination, or feeling; the one who can never be controlled or manipulated; but who, despite this and because of it, is ever graciously and powerfully present to you. *Trust that presence, walk in it, undergo it.*'

In the Protestant tradition, we let God be God, we live in holy fear of God, and we let God be our justification, when we live in a way that respects that.

112

Where talk and concern centres around money, food, entertainment, sports, sex, and health – there is little sense that the earth is ablaze with the fire of God; and even less of a sense that one should have his or her shoes off before it. In that consciousness, our normal consciousness, whenever we do approach God, even in formal prayer and in our churches, we approach God with very measured expectations, a limited agnosticism, and an incapacity to be astonished. The God who is met in the measured expectations of our own desires and imaginative constructs dies in his own impotence and irrelevance. God dies when God's holiness is denied.

Annie Dillard, in the passage quoted at the beginning of this chapter, echoes Karl Barth when she suggests that our faith would be immeasurably purified if God were to blast our religious services (not to mention our conceptions of him) to bits. The Protestant contemplative tradition suggests that God is dead in our lives precisely because we do not let God do that to us. God lives and gives us the preciousness, significance, and immortality we so deeply yearn for only when, through holy fear, we give that God the space within which to truly be God.

Notes

1) Annie Dillard, *Holy the Firm*, NY, 1977, p. 59.
2) Isaiah 55:8–9
3) Job 38–40.
4) Romans 1–8.
5) This is a paraphrase of G. K. Chesterton, *The Everlasting Man*, pp. 26–28.
6) The 4th Lateran Council (1215) taught that the difference between God and creature is always greater than are the similarities between them. 'INTER CREATOREM ET CREATURAM NON POTEST TANTA SIMILITUDO NOTARI QUIN INTER EOS MAJOR SIT DIS SIMILITUDO NOTANDA'. (Denzinger-Banwart, *Enchiridion*, 11th ed., no. 432.)
7) Isaiah 6:3.
8) Luke 15:11–32.
9) Matthew 20:1–16.
10) Luke 10:25–37.
11) John Shea, 'The Indiscriminate Host', in *Stories of Faith*, Chicago, 1980, p. 175.
12) Harold Kushner, *When Bad Things Happen to Good People*, Bobbs-Merrill, Indianapolis, 1961.
13) R. Rubenstein, reflecting upon the unparalleled sin and inhumanity of

Auschwitz, comments: 'When I say we live in a time of the death of God, I mean that the thread uniting God and man, heaven and earth, has been broken. We stand in a cold, silent, unfeeling cosmos, unaided by any purposeful power beyond our own resources. After Auschwitz, what else can a Jew say about God, except that he is dead?' (*After Auschwitz*, Indianapolis, 1966, p. 49.)

14) Romans 1–8.
15) Alan Jones, *Journey into Christ*, NY, 1977, p. 57.
16) Quoted by Jurgen Moltmann, *The Crucified God*, London, 1974, p. 36.
17) See statement of the 4th Lateran Council, note 6, above.
18) Exodus 3:1–6.
19) A paraphrase of Elizabeth Barrett Browning.
20) Henri Nouwen, *In Memoriam*, Notre Dame, Indiana, 1980, pp. 27–30.
21) John Shea, *Stories of God*, p. 137.
22) Mark 13:28.
23) Job 40:3–5 and 42:1–3 (Jerusalem Bible translation).
24) G. K. Chesterton, *Everlasting Man*, p. 159.
25) Michael Buckley, 'Atheism and Contemplation', pp. 696–697.
26) Job 40–42.
27) Karl Rahner, *Prayers for a Lifetime*, NY, 1989, p. 30.
28) Alan Jones, *Journey into Christ*, p. 57
29) Etty Hillesum, *An Interrupted Life, The Diaries of Etty Hillesum, 1941–1943*, NY, 1981, p. 13.
30) Exodus 3:13–14.

Chapter 6

Recognising and appropriating the experience of contingency: the philosophical tradition of theism

PROOFS FOR THE EXISTENCE OF GOD

> It suffices for things to exist for God to become inevitable. Accord to a point of moss, to the smallest ant, the value of existence, and we cannot escape any longer from the terrifying hands which move us all.[1]

These words capture the central idea of a school of contemplative thought which is commonly referred to as *classical theism*. Their belief is that God is only dead when, in our ordinary lives, we lose the awareness of our own contingency, namely, of our radical dependence upon something beyond ourselves. This is rather abstract however and needs a lot of explanation.

When Nietzsche said that God is dead he was speaking more about the death of God within human awareness than about whether or not God actually exists. Irrespective of whether God does or does not exist, our spontaneous consciousness is normally unaware of that existence. Within our normal day, with business as usual, with all our heartaches and headaches, God is generally absent, *dead* in that sense.

Classical theism would agree with Nietzsche; for the most part, God is dead within our normal consciousness. However the reason for this is not that no God exists to be known, or because our ordinary experience is secular and God can be found only in explicit religious experience (prayer and church), but because we do not perceive our own secular experience properly. When we feel our experience as purely secular it is because we are focused only on one dimension of that experience. Classical theism believes that if we were fully awake to what is contained within our so-called secular experience we would find that God is far from dead. Instead God is the ground, horizon, and author of our every experience.

In suggesting this, classical theism is very similar to the mystical tradition we examined earlier and, for that reason, merits being designated as a *contemplative tradition*. Where the classical theists are different is that their approach is philosophical, abstract, and descriptive rather than religious, pious, and prescriptive. In essence, they are saying this: if we examine carefully ordinary experience, any ordinary experience whatsoever, we will find that, far from being secular, it contains within it as its ultimate ground, God. Put more simply, this tradition believes that, at every second, we and everything in our universe *are* being actively breathed into existence and held in it by God. If God, for one second, stopped actively creating, we and everything in the universe would instantly disappear into nothingness. When we are fully aware of what we are actually experiencing (if we could, in their words, shine a hermeneutical flashlight into our experience so as to see everything that is there) we would then be aware that we, and everything else, are being held in existence at every second by God.

On what basis do they affirm this? Their answer constitutes the rest of this chapter. Before going into a detailed explanation, however, an initial image can be helpful. Imagine a dancer dancing. The dance exists only while it is actually being danced by the dancer. At the very instant that the dancer stops, the dance ceases. This tradition understands human life and all of creation in the same way. We are God's dance, actively being danced each second. If the Dancer, God, stopped dancing for even a split second, all would return again to nothingness.

Contemplative perception, being wide awake to all that is revealed in our experience, shows us this. As one of the primary exponents of this school of thought, Austin Farrer, puts it: when we perceive correctly, what we see is ...

not *the-creature-without-the-creator*
or *the-creator-without-the-creature*
but *the-creature-and-the-creator-in-the-cosmological-
    relationship*.[2]

Put more simply, what Farrer is saying, and what this school
is contending, is that when we see contemplatively we perceive
everything against a divine horizon. Or, as Thomas Aquinas
puts it, when we see correctly, we recognise contingency, and
when we recognise contingency, we have proof for the existence
of God.

The proponents of this idea are usually associated with
philosophy rather than contemplation and they represent a
wide variety of backgrounds and come from very different times in history: Anselm, Thomas Aquinas, Leibnitz,
Spinoza, Descartes, Kant, Etienne Gilson, William Paley, Austin
Farrer, Jacques Maritain, Eric Mascall, Jan Walgrave, Martin
D'Arcy, Bernard Lonergan, Karl Rahner, Paul Tillich, Charles
Hartshorne, Langdon Gilkey, Peter Berger, and Joseph Marechal,
among others. Some of them have been associated with
what has been commonly called 'the proofs for existence of
God'; others have not. Despite immense differences among
their thought, they are part of one tradition, the contemplative tradition being spoken of here, in that all of them
affirm that if we perceive reality properly, this perception brings along with it, however inchoately and darkly,
the sense that ordinary experience is grounded in God
as the ultimate ground of being.

They express this in many different ways and, unfortunately,
in nearly all of the cases that expression is very abstract and
can be quite alien to a mind not trained in formal philosophy
... not to mention that, today, it is often considered alien
by a lot of minds that are trained in philosophy! Since it
is not presupposed that the reader of this has such formal
training we will, in so far as it is possible, attempt here to
step outside of the language of technical philosophy. For this
reason, too, we will be very brief on how proponents of this
try to 'prove the existence of God', since this is philosophically
quite technical, and elaborate at greater length on what mem-
bers of this school would call 'rumours of angels' or 'traces
of ultimacy' within ordinary experience.

117

How can the existence of God be proven? How and where does one see traces of ultimacy within ordinary secular experience? How and where does a divine horizon manifest itself in ordinary experience?

THE ARGUMENT FROM THE OUTSIDE . . .
PROOFS FOR THE EXISTENCE OF GOD

Bernard Lonergan once made the statement that all proofs for the existence of God can be reduced to a single premise: *If reality is intelligible, then God exists!*[3] More simply stated, this is his algebra: *If we, the world, and everything in it, make sense, then there must be a God.*

Throughout the centuries many philosophers have developed elaborate arguments around this, attempting to prove that God exists. Their arguments vary greatly, but, in the end, all of them are based upon, as Lonergan suggests, one premise, if the world makes sense then some ultimate principle, God, must exist to explain it.

For purposes of illustration here, allow me to present just one such argument, that of the English philosopher, William Paley. In a book entitled *Natural Theology: Evidence of the Deity Collected from Appearances of Nature*, published in 1802, he argued basically as follows. Imagine that you are walking down a road when your foot accidentally strikes a stone. The question arises within you: 'Who put this stone here? Can it always have been here? Does it need anything beyond itself to explain itself?' It is easy to think no further about these questions. As far as you are concerned the stone could have been there for ever. Of itself the stone does not seemingly force you to think further about it. Now, imagine a slightly different scene. You are walking along a road when your foot accidentally bumps into a watch. It is ticking and has the correct time. The question arises within you: 'Who put this watch here? Can it always have been here? Does it need anything beyond itself to explain itself?' In this case, our minds will not allow us the simplistic answer that the watch has been lying there for ever and that nobody left it there. Why not? Because it is ticking (which implies that if it had been there for ever it would already have stopped ticking) and because it has intelligent and deliberate design which demands that a certain intelligence built it (blind chance might make stones, but it does not construct watches).

Paley then goes on to simply apply the argument: look at the design in our world and especially at the design within ourselves. The human body with its brain and central nervous system is such an incredible entity of intelligent and deliberate design that one cannot simply look at it and say, as one might in the case of the brute existence of a stone, it does not need anything beyond itself to be here. The intelligent and purposive design of the human body, heart, and mind demand something beyond themselves to explain themselves and that something must be a reality that does not itself need something beyond itself. It must precisely be the ground of all intelligence, purpose, and all existence. In a word, it must be God.

In essence, this is the argument from contingency, expressed by so many different thinkers in so many different ways: things, as we know them, do not fully explain themselves. In the end, only some Ultimate, God, can account for the simple fact of existence. If existence makes sense and is explicable, then God exists.

Moreover, these proofs go on to suggest something else which is more apropos to what is at issue here. According to this tradition, when we perceive things properly, contemplatively, we already see them against this background of ultimacy. Thus, you cannot see a watch without knowing at the same time that there is a watchmaker; you cannot see a dance without seeing at the same time a dancer; you cannot see a creature without also knowing a creator; and you cannot be properly aware of who you really are, that is, a being who does not account for its own existence, without knowing at some level that there is an ultimate being that does account for your existence. In brief, you cannot be perceiving and feeling fully if you are unaware that some Ultimate exists as a ground for all that is.

This must be properly understood, however. These proofs are not to be understood in any way as equations which bind the intellect the way a mathematical formula might. They are not so much demonstrations to the human intellect as they are 'monstrations to contemplative intellection'.[4] What is meant by this curious phrase? An analogy can be useful in explaining this.

The Christian creeds are a set of formulae which, of themselves, do not prove that Christ was divine, that he rose from the dead, and that there is eternal life. They function not as a proof, but as a challenge. They challenge Christian consciousness as it journeys adventurously through history not to veer from the whole truth, to avoid any one-sided and narrowed consciousness concerning Christ. A Christian who finds herself or himself at variance with the creeds must do some serious self-examining. The proofs for the existence of God function in a parallel fashion. A person whose everyday consciousness is experienced as purely secular must ask himself of herself some hard questions: 'Am I optimally open? How pure or muddy is my awareness? Am I too preoccupied with certain things so as to be unaware of others? Am I missing the forest for the trees ... the watchmaker for the watch ... the dancer for the dance ... the wide horizon for the narrow perspective ... and the ultimate for the finite? When I no longer see something is it because it is not there or because I am not present?'

The classical proofs for the existence of God are useful as an invitation and guide to contemplation. According to this tradition, just as Christ left us the invitation to 'recognise him in the breaking of the bread', our very existence invites us perennially to recognise God in our lack of self-sufficiency. This, however, becomes clearer when, in a sense, we turn the arguments inside out so as to see what they *feel* like rather than look like.

THE ARGUMENT FROM THE INSIDE ... THEISM AS AN INVITATION TO CONTEMPLATION

The proponents of classical theism assure us that ordinary experience, if entered into correctly, gives off constant proofs for the existence of God. For them, there is no such thing as purely secular experience. Why then are we not more aware of this? Why then is our experience so perennially and pathologically secular? Why do we not see the creator more when we see the creature?

Their simple answer is that this constitutes a fault in contemplation. God is there to be seen, we just fail to see properly. There are traces of ultimacy in ordinary experience, we stop short of appropriating them. Moreover, we do, in fact, *feel* God, we are just not aware enough of what we are feeling. In brief, our normal experience appears to us as purely secular because we are not sufficiently contemplative within it.

How can this be so? Are they accusing us of being unaware of what is contained within our own experience? In answer to that, they make a key distinction: they distinguish between awareness viewed without a full hermeneutic of experience and awareness viewed within a full hermeneutic of experience. More simply, this is a distinction between non-contemplative awareness and contemplative awareness. The former refers to what we are normally conscious of within our experience and the latter refers to what is contained in our actual experience when examined in all its complexity and totality.

In their view, when we view our experience non-contemplatively it appears to us, save for very rare instances, as secular. It does not point beyond itself to the existence of God, nor does it contain, to use some of their phrases, 'traces of ultimacy', 'rumours of angels', 'hierophanies', 'contuitions of God', or 'a divine horizon'. Conversely, however, their contention is that if we do view our experience contemplatively it does, and infallibly so, bring us to see beyond the dance to the Dancer. It yields always a certain contuition of God. Experience, they contend, examined under the light of a proper hermeneutics, is never secular. We can feel secular only if we are not really in touch with what we are experiencing

Is this true? In our ordinary lives, what do we actually feel? Do we or do we not *feel* God's presence in our ordinary awareness? Is there no purely secular experience?

Classical theism suggests that when one looks at contemporary experience superficially, without examining it with a hermeneutical flashlight, it appears to be largely secular, devoid of any divine horizon. However, if a proper hermeneutic of experience is used so as to uncover those parts which normally lie inchoate and unappropriated, then our everyday experience will show itself to be anything but secular. Contemporary theists like Langdon Gilkey and Peter Berger, among others, would submit that, when all is said and done, we do not *feel* all that secular, but find that our ordinary experience is affected always by a sense of something beyond it, some ultimate which relativises it.

By way of explanation, they illustrate this by analysing how the major characteristics of the so-called secular mindset are, in fact, felt by contemporary persons. Here, they suggest, there is a huge difference between what we commonly *profess* we experience and what we, in fact, *actually* do experience. Our secular version of what is contained in our experience is, not unlike our opinion about ourselves, often quite different from the facts. This difference, they say, is flushed out by shining a certain flashlight into our experience. This flashlight, they submit, shows that we do not, in fact, experience ourselves as secular, that is, without a god (CONTINGENT), without absolutes (RELATIVE), mortal (TRANSIENT), and under no obligation of obedience to something higher than ourselves (AUTONOMY) – as the creed of secularity would have us believe. Examined more closely, our experience reveals something quite different.

With this in mind, we examine their analysis of this in some detail:

1) *Secular experience seen non-contemplatively, without the aid of a hermeneutical flashlight*

The so-called secular mindset, in its self-understanding, often defines itself by four major characteristics, CONTINGENCY, RELATIVITY, TRANSIENCE, and AUTONOMY. How does it, in what it espouses about itself, understand these?

i) Contingency

The secular mindset would have us believe that the immediate is all that there is, existence begins and ends with the here and now.

In this view, the human person and the cosmos are not the result of a deliberate and loving act of a God. The universe is not seen to have any ultimate principle of purpose, order, or coherence. Rather, beyond the here and now, there lies nothing ultimate, no explanation, no reason, no final plan or purpose. Existence just is and it can be described and that is all! Everything is an accident.

Langdon Gilkey aptly summarises this position. Secularism sees us as 'set within a universe with neither a transcendent source nor an inherent or ultimate order; our nature is constituted exhaustively by blind nature or a meaningless void, not hostile, to be sure, but empty of purpose, indifferent, a faceless mystery. We can talk about it only in terms of the immediately given patterns of our phenomenal experience of it; beyond that we can know and speak nothing meaningful about what is.'[5] George Santayana expresses the same idea poetically: 'Matter is the invisible wind which, sweeping for no reason over the field of essences, raises some of them into a cloud of dust: and that whirlwind we call existence ... and, in such a world, necessity is a conspiracy of accidents.'[6]

ii) Relativity
In the secular mindset the idea is present that we experience our existence as relative, namely, that within our experience we find nothing as absolute, normative, and non-negotiable. There are no absolute oughts.

Adherents of secularism contend that all of our experience is pinioned within the flow of change and history, determined by what lies behind it, shaped by what surrounds it, and replaced by what follows it. Their contention is that everything in our universe is essentially interrelated and, thus, must be understood solely in terms of the nexus of relationships out of which it has been formed, rather than in relationship to anything transcendent to it. Everything is simply a product of nature and change. There is nothing outside of nature and history, that is, nothing that is underived, unchanging, and self-sufficient. In a word, there is no absolute.

iii) Transience
A key prong in the self-definition of the secular mindset is that we experience ourselves and everything else as mortal and transient. Secular experience, they assure us, affirms that *all is in time and is due to die*. Nothing will last, all is time-bound between birth and death. Accordingly, the relevant environment for our hopes and fears is confined to what is contained within this life. Concepts such as 'for ever', 'next life', 'eternity', and 'kingdom of God beyond history' have no meaning beyond expressing naive wishing. There is only this life and all meaningful hope works within those parameters.

iv) Autonomy

Finally, proponents of secularity would have us believe that, today, except for a certain guilt neurosis which many of us carry over from our religious past, we feel the freedom to shape our lives according to our own choices for meaning as opposed to having to live out some form of obedience to a God above us. We find ourselves in this life, they say, as self-creative, meant to decide for ourselves the meaning of existence. Values are not lived out because of the wishes or plan of some transcendent deity, or because we are given a vocation from something antecedent to ourselves which we must respect and submit ourselves to, but because they can be freely chosen to give meaning to our lives. We are our own project, called to creativity, not obedience.

In this spirit, obedience, submission, and self-surrender to something sensed as being above us or beyond us is seen as either a naivete or as a lack of nerve in the face of truth. We are on our own, so it is professed, and there is no need to refer our behaviour to courts above our own. Concomitant with this belief, there is often a certain aggressiveness towards anything that would suggest obedience or a lack of free choice. The suggestion that one must be obedient to a transcendent God, or to some transcendent norms, is considered an affront to the contemporary mindset.

In summary, we see that the ideology of secularism would have us believe that our ordinary experience tells us that this world is all that there is. It, alone, is relevant in terms of hope, purpose, moral choice, and fulfilment. There are no absolutes. There is no for ever, or next-life. We wake up in this world as orphans, all on our own. There is no great creator and parent in the sky who can help us and to whom we owe obedience. Our lives are, in the end, shaped *only* by the accidents of history, the web of our interrelationships, what this life can offer, and the meaning we can give to ourselves through our free choices. We find ourselves, in this world, truly on our own.

For some proponents of secularity, this is viewed positively and optimistically, namely, as an opportunity finally to be free of the asphyxiating dictates of a non-existent God and his very existent clerics. For them, it is a chance to finally come of age, to grow up. For others, such as Albert Camus, this is viewed negatively. If there is no God, we are orphaned, pathetically abandoned, robbed of deep meaning, final significance, and the ultimate loving graciousness which alone could vindicate love and make life worth living. In either case, however, the bottom-line is the same: ordinary experience does not contain traces of ultimacy or set us against a divine horizon. It sets us face to face with the one normative fact that there is, namely, that we, and everything else that is, are contingent, relative, transient, and on our own!

But is this the true picture? Do we in fact experience ourselves and the world in this sense?

The proponents of classical theism submit that this is *not* in fact what we actually experience. According to them, when one examines everyday experience more closely (with a good flashlight) one sees that what we espouse about the secularity of our experience and what in fact goes on inside our experience are two very different things.

2) *Secular experience seen contemplatively, with the aid of a hermeneutical flashlight*

Classical theism asserts that when we examine our actual experience closely we see that what is expressed in the philosophy of secularism is quite simply not true. Instead, in every meaningful experience we have, we sense, however unconsciously, some absolute which grounds what we are experiencing and relativises it. Ordinary experience, classical theism assures us, is full of hierophanies, rumours of angels, and traces of transcendence. God is anything but dead in secular experience.

Where do we experience God within our secular experience? In order to illustrate this, they turn, armed with a hermeneutical flashlight, to re-examine the idea that ordinary experience tells us that we are contingent, relative, transient, and autonomous in this world.

i) Contingency ... revisited

When we examine very closely our own experience we see that, at one level, it seems that this world and what it offers are all that is real and important, that any purpose and meaning we can give our lives must be taken from them, and that they alone are the relevant sphere for our hopes. At another level, however, our actual experience belies that. In nearly all of our ordinary actions, we experience something beyond the purely immediate, the here and now. We, much to our own consternation at times, find ourselves facing something much larger than the immediate here and now. This is experienced in two ways: negatively, as ultimate threat; and positively, as ultimate graciousness and gratuity.

Negatively, we experience this when we, at times, experience feelings of helplessness, dependency, emptiness, terror, void, and threat which are entirely out of proportion to what is contained within our immediate experience. Unlike neurosis and other obsessions which can also trigger deep feelings of void beyond what the present situation merits, this experience is marked by its ultimate character. It does not just cause deep pain in one area, it totally relativises every area and leaves us with the feeling that everything in the here and now is flimsy and not very important. There is a dim sense that there is something beyond the here and now whose reality dwarfs the here and now. But what is beyond?

If we believe that there is nothing, no God, no ultimate foundation or meaning to existence, then it is nothingness itself which takes on the character of an ultimate and forces our horizon beyond the here and now. An infinite void becomes a god before which everything we are and do is threatened in an ultimate way.

When we feel this void, we sense ourselves precisely as standing before an ultimate. However, here God is experienced, not as a final principle which creates and sustains us, but as a final threat which can extinguish us. Nonetheless, in such an experience, there is the sense of something absolute, something which totally relativises everything else.

Moreover, this experience is not uncommon and it is had by persons of all ages. We use expressions such as 'keeping the demons at bay' and few and lucky are those persons who never find their ordinary lives, both in their waking hours and in their dreams, relativised and sometimes terrorised by the sense of standing before an absolute void.

Inevitably, before such a threat, we search desperately for some positive ultimate, for some gracious god who can steady our lives. We then either find God, create idols, or we end up in despair. Ordinary existence, entirely independent of any explicit religious considerations, forces that choice on us – God or despair! We are simply unable to live for very long merrily on the basis of the here and now. Absolute void and, as we shall see, absolute graciousness consistently subvert our attempts to simply live, love, and hope on the basis of the immediate. Without being invited in, some god inevitably casts a threatening shadow or a gracious light into our present moment and, for this reason, we never have purely secular experience.

Positively, this is experienced in bursts of life which are inexplicable purely in terms of the here and now. In our ordinary day-to-day experience, there is present, as the very foundation of all we are and do, a sense of joy, vitality, meaning, and strength which is only explicable by something beyond the immediate. When we are not clinically depressed there is, precisely, present always the sense that our lives and the whole universe are good and have meaning because, at their deepest level, they are being buoyed up and continually refuelled by some ultimate gracious power.

This is something we feel more than think. It manifests itself unconsciously in our vitality and in our valuing of persons, things, and ourselves. In a word, it manifests itself as *health*. We have the feeling, no matter how dimly this is present, that it is good to be alive. As Langdon Gilkey puts it:

> We all love our own being, our existence, our life. Humans are aware of many joys, of course, but underneath all of them there is the exultation in being alive, in feeling and using one's powers – of sensing, smelling, eating, loving, using one's body. Here we experience the sheer joy of being and existing: here the reality and power of *existence* are felt from the inside as joyful vitality. And this inner and most vital joy is the centre and ground of all valuing; it provides the most basic reason for existing, though it is much more a fundamental tone to our being in the world than it is a rational reason.[7]

Moreover, this sense of the goodness of existence which ultimately undergirds our health and vitality, is experienced as given to us, as uncreated by ourselves, as *gift*.

127

The sociologist of religion, Peter Berger, gives an excellent illustration of how this works. For him, the simplest and most ordinary of experiences, seen under a hermeneutical flashlight, reveal a God who is the gracious foundation of the here and now and without whom the here and now does not make sense. Thus he cites as an example the simple action of a mother comforting a frightened child in the night. In this action he sees an implicit act of faith:

> Consider the most ordinary, and probably the most fundamental, of all – the ordinary gesture by which a mother reassures her anxious child.
> A child wakes up in the night, perhaps from a bad dream, and finds himself surrounded by darkness, alone, beset by nameless threats. At such a moment the contours of trusted reality are blurred and invisible. In the terror of incipient chaos the child cries out for his mother. It is hardly an exaggeration to say that, at this moment, the mother is being invoked as a high priestess of protective order. It is she (and, in many cases, she alone) who has the power to banish the chaos and to restore the benign shape of the world. And, of course, any good mother will do just that. She will take the child and cradle him in the timeless gesture of the Magna Mater who became our Madonna. She will turn on a lamp, perhaps, which will encircle the scene with a warm glow of reassuring light. She will speak or sing to the child and the content of this communication will invariably be the same – 'Don't be afraid – everything is in order, everything is all right.'[8]

The mother's comforting reassurance, 'Don't be afraid, it is all right', is, in fact, a profession of faith. When she says these words, she is making an act of faith just as surely, if not as explicitly, as if she were saying: 'I believe in God, the Almighty, the creator of heaven and earth who made existence good and whose love and redemptive power will, in the end, assure that goodness ... and so you can trust!'

When she reassures the child that there is nothing to be frightened about, she means it, and she means it (without her even realising this) not so much on the basis that there are no immediate dangers to the child, as on the basis that, *ultimately*, we are all in the hands of graciousness and love and not in the hands of maliciousness and terror. And she believes this not so much on the basis of any explicit religious consideration, but on the basis of something *given* to her along with her ordinary perception and awareness, namely, the sense that, in the end, everything is all right because the dance of creation, despite all its present groaning, is being danced by an all-good and all-loving Dancer.

This, classical theism would submit, is what ordinary experience reveals when it is fully flushed out by the beam of a good hermeneutical flashlight, that is, by proper contemplativeness. Far from finding that the here and now is the relevant environment for our hopes, we find instead that there is no neutral middle ground on which to simply experience the here and now, without ultimate graciousness or ultimate void invading and colouring the experience. Unlike animals, we are not afforded the opportunity to munch our food contentedly and be happy or restless on that basis. Our ordinary lives are buoyed up or relativised by hope or despair which have their roots in something deeper and more fundamental than just what is contained in the immediate situation. Whether or not at any given minute we feel that everything is all right or is not all right depends more upon what kinds of traces of ultimacy we are experiencing than upon what is more superficially present to us in that given moment.

The present moment does not come to us devoid of colouring by an absolute. In all our ordinary experiences there are hierophanies, rumours of angels, and traces of ultimacy. Ordinary awareness is not so ordinary. Rather it contains always, dimly and sometimes not-so-dimly, the sense that beneath, above, and inside this dance there is a Dancer whose ultimate graciousness or nothingness and malevolence is what really gives this moment meaning. The present moment comes to us as threatened or graced by something beyond it. This is what is affirmed in the proofs for the existence of God and what is *felt* in them when they are turned inside out.

ii) Relativity ... revisited

The expressed philosophy of secularism would have us believe that we experience everything as simply relative, that nothing presents itself to us as absolute, eternal, normative, permanent, and non-negotiable. Is this true? Is this, in fact, our experience?

Again, classical theism submits that our true experience reveals the opposite. We do not live our lives as if nothing was absolute. Rather, in our lives, and habitually so, we find that we cannot operate (make decisions, motivate ourselves, or find meaning) except by relating ourselves to an absolute.

We experience this in our inability to live without a TELEOLOGY which relates us precisely to an absolute. What does this mean? Let me attempt to explain this rather abstract notion and then illustrate it with some examples.

Animals live largely by instinct, by genetic programming. They do not have to struggle for meaning. For them, to a very large extent, meaning comes from biological programming, pure and simple.

In humans, the biological instincts are much weaker and we must live and find meaning beyond genetic programming. Accordingly, we choose actions and consciously design patterns of behaviour so as to find meaning. In choosing behaviour, we find that, for our lives to have meaning, we must act in such a way that our actions are not just a succession of events related only by chance and accident, but they must construct a meaningful *pattern* of behaviour. When there is no pattern to our actions then we experience meaninglessness.

Moreover, for there to be a meaningful pattern to our actions there must be *one thread* that somehow relates all our actions to each other and dyes them all with a common colour of meaning. We construct this thread by, first of all, connecting ourselves to some end, some destiny (a soteriology), something that we sense will give us final meaning. From this *telos*, we then draw a string backwards and that string, anchored to that final destiny, then functions as the thread that binds all our actions into one meaningful whole. If that thread breaks, or if the end point shifts or is no longer considered as absolute, we have a crisis of meaning.

Simply put, we cannot live meaningfully without a teleology, and we create a teleology for ourselves *only* by relating ourselves to something that functions as an absolute anchor, as normative in terms of meaning. Hence, secular experience is not, in the end, so secular after all. Instead we find that, irrespective of explicit religious commitment, we live our lives always in relationship to, and ultimately in worship of, an absolute.

Freud once said that we understand the anatomy of things best if we can look at them when they are broken. With this in mind, it is interesting to look at what happens when someone tries to live life without such an absolute. In those instances, life and the many experiences within it become meaningless.

We see a poignant illustration of this in Albert Camus' novel, *L'etranger*.[9] His anti-hero, Meursault, is a young man who works as a clerk in Algiers. He lives in the usual manner of a young middle-class bachelor: cooking his own meals, sleeping with his girlfriend, holidaying at weekends, drinking with his friends, reading and going to the cinema. However, since he does not believe in God and sees no absolute anywhere, he cannot because of this very fact find any real meaning or reason to do anything, including loving or hating. Judging everything to be relative, he can find no real meaning for his life. All his actions then become nothing more than a meaningless succession of events without any purpose, destiny, or significance, done in complete indifference. When his girlfriend asks him: 'Do you love me?' he answers that he supposes he doesn't but, in any case, he sees no meaning whatever to the question. When she asks whether he would consent to marry her, he answers that he does not care one way or the other, but he would marry her if she would like that. He eventually kills a man, without passion or hatred and even without any great reason for doing it. He is condemned to be executed and faces the execution with complete indifference. Nothing whatsoever, living, loving, dying, helping friends, or the death of a family member can be a matter of more than comfort or inconvenience. All is simply relative.

However, we all know that, barring some rare depressed and stoic exceptions, nobody in fact lives with the indifference of Camus' *L'etranger*. Rather, irrespective of explicit belief in God, people create for themselves a teleology which holds their lives together, motivates them, gives them a sense of purpose and destiny, and has them loving and hating with some zest.

Further, when we examine the teleologies we do create for ourselves, we find that the absolute that we pick to connect our destiny and meaning to them becomes the normative criterion against which all value is measured. Thus, for example, many persons, while rejecting any explicit belief in God or any other absolute, will invariably set up as normative certain ideals – political, cultural, moral, humanitarian, educational, aesthetic – and then proceed to invest these (for example, Marxism, personal development, social justice, sexual fulfilment, concern for the environment, health of one's body) with an absoluteness and sacredness that mimics and parallels every movement of religion, including the accusation of sacrilege against anyone who treats with irreverence what is so sacredly cherished. These ideals, which invariably become ideologies and idols, function as surrogate gods and, as such, become the anchor for the thread which holds life together and gives it meaning.

We need constantly to refer ourselves to an absolute not just to motivate us at a very basic level, beyond the depression and indifference of Camus' *L'etranger*, but also to provide the proper *symbolic hedge* to surround our actions. Two very clear examples can be used to illustrate this, the experience of waiting and the experience of sexuality.

Waiting is an essential and characteristic part of life. We live habitually in restlessness, unfulfilled, yearning, unconsummated, waiting, waiting for someone or something to arrive that will fulfil us. Normally, however, this tension can be endured and is part of a hope we live with, namely, we have some sense of destiny and are waiting for certain things which will, we sense, eventually bring that about. In this case, waiting is a meaningful activity because we are waiting under a certain symbolic hedge; there is, in fact, something to wait for, our destiny. We then experience the flow of time meaningfully, despite our tension and incompleteness.

However, when we are deprived of a reference to an absolute which can give us this sense of destiny, waiting becomes absurd and loses all meaning. This is brilliantly illustrated by Samuel Beckett in his play, *Waiting for Godot*.

The play centres on two old tramps, Vladimir and Estragon, who are waiting for a Mr Godot, with whom they vaguely believe themselves to have an appointment. However it is evident that Mr Godot is never going to arrive. Their waiting, since it has no ultimate purpose and is, in a manner of speaking, destiny-less, is also pointless and absurd. Time itself becomes problematic, weighs heavy, and becomes a meaningless burden.

What is illustrated here by Samuel Beckett is first cousin to what Camus depicts in *L'etranger*: without reference to some absolute, life itself cannot be rendered meaningful. For Camus' Meursault, there is nothing that can ultimately motivate and give meaning; for Beckett's stood-up tramps, there is no meaningful way to pass the time. For classical theism, this is what the proofs for the existence of God *feel* like when they are turned both inside out and reversed. Thus, in a manner of speaking the doctrine of the absurdity of the world is simply what the doctrine of the contingency of the world becomes when it is transposed from a theistic to an atheistic setting.

What is true for the experience of *waiting* is also true for the experience of *sexuality*. All understandings of it that strip away its teleological and symbolic hedge and reduce it to a simple here and now experience, devoid of dimensions of ultimacy and sacredness, serve to render it ambiguous and depreciate what it has to offer. When sexual encounter is not related, however inchoately, to ultimate destiny and meaning, it remains pleasurable, as does eating a good meal, but it now becomes ambiguous and, even at its best, loses much of its power to trigger depth and create union beyond fleeting sensation.

Doris Lessing, in her five-volume series on Martha Quest, explores brilliantly this theme. Her heroine, Martha, rejects belief in God and also, save for brief periods of her life, rejects investing anything else with dimensions of ultimacy and sacredness either. Her ensuing struggle to find a teleology which binds her life into one meaningful whole is extremely enlightening, particularly as she struggles to comprehend and find meaning in her sexuality. For Martha, sex is contingent in that it does not point to anything beyond itself. Accordingly it eventually loses all reference to destiny, depth, significant meaning, and, at last, even to love itself. Devoid of the umbrella that a connection to destiny can provide, it becomes an ambiguous and superficial experience:

> Sex: sensation pulsing on the current of blood and breath. Heartbeat-heart: separate. Heart with emotions, 'love', but isolated and looked at like this, a small thing, a pulse of little feeling, like an animal impulse towards

another, a warmth. Sex, heart, the currents of the automatic body ...

She understood that it was this that had sent Mark up to Martha to make love. What an extraordinary phrase that was, 'make love'. Love, love ... Martha sat listening, while the word 'love' exploded and bred, and thought of the act in which she had engaged so very many times and with different people: she could see Martha, in different shapes, and sizes, according to the time, her limbs moving, enlaced with this man, that man, always the same way, or so it looked from where she was now, but subjectively, putting herself back inside the act, it was not possible to use the same words for what she felt. Mark, when he had come upstairs, possessed by some explosive force which gripped her now, and had made love, made sex, made something, had used a different energy from what Jack had used, all that time ago when he used their two bodies like conductors or conduits for the force which moved and lifted them to – she could not remember where ... She was sitting and muttering as she had years before: We don't understand the first thing about what goes on, not the first thing, 'make love', 'make sex', 'orgasms', 'climaxes' – it was all nonsense, words, sounds, invented by half-animals who understood nothing at all. Great forces as impersonal as thunder or lightning or sunlight or the movement of oceans being contracted and heaved and rolled in their beds by the moon, swept through bodies, and now she knew quite well why Mark had come blindly upstairs to the nearest friendly body, being in the grip of this force or *a* force, one of them. Not sex. Not necessarily. Not unless one chose to make it so.

Jack had once said: 'The thousand volts'. He had been talking of hate. 'The thousand volts of hatred.' A thousand volts of love? A thousand volts of – compassion? Of charity?[10]

In this passage, Lessing gives us a description of what secular experience feels like when it is, precisely, not related to any absolute. We see that sexuality, like existence itself, cannot be rendered meaningful unless, within it, there is already some awareness of a connection to some absolute. Like Camus and Beckett, Lessing shows that unless we grasp 'the-dance-in-relationship-to-the-Dancer' we are unable to make much sense of the dance.

An obvious objection can be raised here, namely that of Feuerbach and Marx: the fact that we cannot find meaning in life without reference to an absolute does not mean such an absolute exists. Proving that we would want and need a God is not the same thing as proving that such a God exists.

That critique, however valid in many other contexts, misses a critical point in the argument here. What these examples illustrate is not so much the fact that we need a God as the fact that *we function spontaneously in the light of the fact that we have already apprehended one*. What is strained and artificially contrived is not the sense that we and our actions are related to some absolute, but the totally *a-theistic* characters of Camus, Beckett, and Lessing. The Martha Quests, Meursaults, Vladimirs and Estragons exist more in the pages of literature and philosophical speculation (and in clinical depression) than in normal life. In real life, there is present, as the very sign of health itself, the congenital inability to accept for very long meaninglessness. That chronic rejection of meaninglessness is what the principle of the philosophical principle of sufficient reason feels like psychologically. It is also what the proofs for the existence of God feel like when they are reversed and turned inside out.

iii) Transience ... revisited
Do we really live our lives as if all is in time and all is due to die? Do we really believe that the relevant environment for our hopes and fears is merely this present life?

Again, when we place our experience under the revealing light of a good hermeneutical flashlight we see that our actual experience comes laden with dimensions that make a tranquil acceptance of mortality impossible. Our felt existence belies our espoused beliefs. We live meaningful lives only by not accepting mortality and transience. We refuse death at its every turn.

At a more superficial level, this manifests itself in three ways:

a) IN OUR COMPULSION TO LEAVE A MARK. So much of what we do derives from the drive for immortality. We cannot stand the knowledge that we are merely animals that live and die and that, in the end, death and insignificance is our lot. In our depths there is something that radically rejects this and we act out accordingly. We attempt to guarantee some kind of immortality for ourselves: set a world record, become famous, have a child, write a book. Inside each of us there is the congenital propensity to leave some permanent mark.

b) IN OUR REFUSAL TO REALLY FACE THE FACT OF OUR OWN DEATH. Even as we say the words: 'Someday I will die!', we do not really accept them. We have a death-denying mechanism inside us which simply blocks out what is implied in saying that we will die. Others around us die. Accidents, cancer, diseases, old age, do death's reaping, but death always takes others, never us. Somehow, even as we theoretically know that we will die, another part of us knows that this is not true. Others die, we don't!

c) IN OUR REFUSAL TO EVER ACCEPT THAT WE HAVE REACHED OUR ZENITH. Not only do we refuse to accept that we will die, but we refuse too to ever accept that our lives, at any point, are as good as they will ever get. Our minds and hearts, unconsciously and consciously, refuse to ever accept that any point of life is ever the limit of our growth and development. Even when, in terms of our practical hopes, we are (in the literal sense of that colloquial expression) 'over the hill', we know at some other level that we are not, that in terms of real life we are still babies and what we yearn to attain in terms of love, creativity, achievement, and significance is still in our future. Never do we accept any present as the highest, most significant, healthiest, and happiest moment we will ever experience.

Most radically, though, we experience our refusal of death in our experience of hope. We possess an astonishing capacity to hope in the face of any situation, no matter how practically hopeless it is. When we are surrounded by death on all sides, our inmost being says a resounding *No* to death in a most radical way. We hope, we affirm life and ultimate graciousness, irrespective of how practically awful any concrete historical situation might be. A powerful example of this can be seen in the words that a prisoner, about to be executed by the Nazis during the Second World War, wrote on a concentration camp wall:

I believe in the sun, even when it isn't shining
I believe in love, even when I feel it not
I believe in God, even when he is silent

On what basis do we as humans possess this stunning capacity to affirm graciousness and love as the heart of reality when the here and now demands the opposite affirmation?

The answer to that can only be that, somehow, we apprehend in the here and now, despite its often brutal suggestion that death and darkness are the final answer, some gracious absolute which is beyond. Like the classical theist who looks at a rose or a stone and is able to perceive in its contingency the creator and sustainer who is giving it existence at that precise moment, so too do we in our experience of hope sense a gracious Dancer who is still Lord over all dances, including the horrible one that now threatens us, and who will bring us all to a new day and an ultimately loving dance.

iv) Autonomy ... revisited

Do we really believe that we no longer need to submit to some transcendent lord to whom we owe obedience in holy fear? Does the human person today, as the non-contemplative ideology of ourselves would contend, feel confident to create his or her own meaning, independent of obeying some transcendent will? In the end, do we really feel liberated, free, autonomous, no longer under the dominion of a God?

Again, when we examine our actual feelings and behaviour we see a huge difference between the ideology which proclaims our autonomy and our actual felt experience and concrete behaviour. In real life, we experience our freedom as conditioned, and as conditioned by some absolute lord who, while demanding obedience, promises redemption. How is this so?

Put simply, we experience our freedom as ambiguous, flawed,

and in need of redemption and as conscienced, and in need of a lord. But this needs elaboration.

First of all, we experience our freedom as ambiguous and flawed. Like Paul, any sensitive person experiences his or her freedom as something of which they are not fully in control and for whose moral impotence and failings they, ultimately, need redemption: 'I cannot understand my own behaviour. I fail to carry out the things I want to do, and find myself doing the very things I hate ... with the result that instead of doing the good things I want to do, I carry out the sinful things I do not want.'[11]

Those words of Paul have a universal ring to them. All sensitive persons know that, inside them, there are insoluble and inexplicable levels of complexity, hypocrisy, and moral impotence which render them incapable much of the time of living out their own ideals. Leonard Bernstein, in his *Mass*, gives a poetic description of this:

> What I say I don't feel
> What I feel I don't show
> What I show isn't real
> What is real, Lord – I don't know
> No, no, no – I don't know.
>
> I don't know why every time
> I find a new love I wind up destroying it.
> I don't know why I'm
> So freaky-minded, I keep on kind of enjoying it –
> Why I drift off to sleep
> With pledges of deep resolve again,
> Then along comes the day
> And suddenly they dissolve again –
> I don't know ...
>
> What I need I don't have
> What I have I don't own
> What I own I don't want
> What I want, Lord, I don't know.[12]

Another such expression of the flawedness of human

autonomy, that rings true universally, is found in the words of Anna Blaman:

> I realised that it is simply impossible for a human being to be and remain 'good' or 'pure'. If, for instance, I wanted to be attentive in one direction, it could only be at the cost of neglecting another. If I gave my heart to one thing, I left another in the cold ... No day and no hour goes by without my being guilty of some inadequacy. We never do enough, and what we do is never well enough done ... except being inadequate, which we are good at, because it is the way we are made. This is true of me and of everyone else. Every day and every hour brings with it its weight of moral guilt, as regards my work and relations with others ... I am constantly catching myself out in my human failings, and in spite of their being implied in my human imperfections, I am conscious of a sort of check. And this means that my human shortcomings are also my human guilt. It sounds strange that we should be guilty where we can do nothing about it. But even where there is no purpose, or deliberate intention, we have a conviction of our own shortcomings, and of consequent guilt, a guilt which sometimes shows itself all too clearly in the consequences of what we have done or left undone.[13]

These expressions by St Paul, Leonard Bernstein, and Anna Blaman, are not expressions of neurosis but are sensitive renderings of a universal human experience, namely, that as free beings we function in a very ambiguous and flawed manner and we yearn for a certain redemption from our own moral impotence. This points to the fact that human freedom is partly mystery and that, in the end, it cannot be rendered fully intelligible in purely secular terms but needs the broken language of religion which ties autonomy to the categories of redemption, original sin, justification, grace, and atonement. Against these categories our freedom can be rendered intelligible and lived with creatively. Devoid of them, autonomy becomes unintelligible and we become, in the words of existential philosophy, an absurdity.

To live happily in freedom, we need a Redeemer. Our actual experience of freedom, daily, teaches us this.

In the flawedness of our own freedom we experience our radical dependence upon God and, more importantly, *already* experience inchoately redemption by that God. In a paraphrase of Austin Farrer, what we experience is not the flawedness and ambiguity of freedom's dance, but the flawedness and ambiguity of freedom's dance being redeemed by an ultimately gracious Dancer.

Further still, we *experience our freedom as conscienced and in need of a lord.* We do not experience our freedom as absolute, or as arbitrary. Rather, simply put, in our experience of freedom we find ourselves always before a tribunal which, under analysis, reveals itself to be infinite, absolute, and personal, and which demands our obedience and worship. Freedom is always experienced in relationship to some lord.

Dan Berrigan puts it more existentially when he writes: 'I have been searching for years for someone to be obedient to. That is a conservative statement, a profoundly traditional one, and so I mean it. For I am persuaded, in Simone Weil's phrase, that obedience is a need of the soul; that, without proper scope and corrected shape and admonitory word, we languish and inflate and grow foolish, even to ourselves.'[14]

Doris Lessing, in her *Golden Notebook*, also illustrates this. Her heroine, Anna, tries in a serious way to live out the philosophy that would have us believe that the human person has come of age and is now free of all need for obedience to anything transcendent. Her Anna is a very gifted writer. She also possesses an abundance of intelligence, attractiveness, and money. She has virtually everything going for her. Yet as she attempts to live as a fully liberated person, slowly, she senses that her personality is disintegrating and she can give no possible explanation as to why. The book ends, as it begins, with Lessing proclaiming: 'It's all very odd, isn't it?'[15] Lessing submits throughout this work that the human personality falls apart unless it finds some lord, however that might be conceived. Left totally on our own, without any absolute tribunal to which to relate our freedom, our lives slowly become unintelligible, odd, even to ourselves.

Langdon Gilkey, in his analysis of this, shows how the axiom, *what is natural to us is not atheism but idolatry*, is so spontaneously played out in our contemporary world.[16] His analysis points out how all of us, whether we admit it or not, serve some lord, some real or surrogate God. Our freedom simply finds itself unable to operate meaningfully without genuflecting before some absolute, be that Yahweh, Allah, Krishna, Brahmin, Mother Earth, some ideology, an astrological sign, the harmony of the planets, universal love, some ideal within aesthetics, the beauty of the human body, the power of romance or sex, or some political, social, moral, or ecological cause. Everyone invests something with the attributes of God and then lives obediently to that lord and sacrifices and worships accordingly. Human freedom simply does not operate in isolation from obedience to some absolute. As many a poet has put it, we find salvation in surrender.

And, as we see from looking at this, not only does our freedom have within it the congenital propensity for obedience to some lord, it spontaneously and habitually moves us as well towards worship. We, as Chesterton so aptly puts it, feel ourselves most truly free and truly human when we are kneeling in submission. Analysing pagan worship, he writes:

(There is) a thing very deep in humanity indeed ... This deep truth of the danger of insolence, or being too big for our boots, runs through all the great Greek tragedies and makes them great ...
The crux and crisis is that we find it natural to worship; even natural to worship unnatural things. The posture of the idol might be stiff and strange; but the gesture of worship is generous and beautiful. We not only feel freer when we bend, we actually feel taller when we bow. Henceforth anything that takes away the gesture of worship stunts and even maims us forever. Henceforth being merely secular is servitude and inhibition. If we cannot pray we are gagged; if we cannot kneel we are in iron.[17]

We feel most free when we are worshipping. Chesterton adds that, in the ordinary gesture of prayer, it is normal and necessary

141

that our hands are lifted up, but, he contends, it is no less a parable that our hands are empty!

We see therefore that the ordinary experience of freedom brings with it, however little this might be explicitly acknowledged, the propensity for obedience to and worship of some absolute. We are incurably conscienced, incurably drawn to self-surrender in obedience, and incurably drawn to worship. In our freedom, always, we sense ourselves as standing before a God. To again paraphrase Austin Farrer: we experience our free dance in relationship to the Lord of the dance ... to whose rhythm we sense that we must adjust our steps!

CONTEMPLATION AS NOT TAKING THE WORLD FOR GRANTED

'We shall never become theists if we take the world for granted; but so long as we do not take it for granted we are within measurable distance of taking it as granted us by God.'[18]

These words by Eric Mascall summarise the contemplative *praxis* of classical theism. Their language about proofs for the existence of God is not an attempt to produce some mathematical-type equations which force anyone to believe. Classical theism is, instead, a school of thought which invites one to contemplate existence in a certain way. Its syllogisms are prescriptions for contemplation.

Simply put, those prescriptions can be reduced to a single one: *Appropriate your contingency!* Be aware of what is gift in your life. Be alert to, and searingly honest in accepting, all that you find present in your experience and you will find that you are not a self-sufficient being but that, at each second of your life, you are being created, sustained, challenged, and redeemed by some absolute beyond you.

When Nietzsche's madman proclaimed that God is dead, he, in the view of classical theism, was not announcing that no God exists beyond the here and now, but that, in the here and now, we have become so engrossed with the marketplace and business as usual (narcissism, pragmatism, and excessive distraction) that we have begun to take their existence for granted

... and, when the sense of gift is lost, we concomitantly experience the death of the Giver!

At the end of Luke's gospel, Christ invites us to 'recognise him in the breaking of the bread', in eucharist. Eucharist means thanksgiving. Thanksgiving and gratitude follow upon the recognition of gift. Classical theism, as a contemplative tradition, invites us to recognise God in the experience of being gifted (for that is what contingency means). When we see our lives correctly, we see that all is gift. If we appropriate this, then our eyes will be opened and we will recognise that God has been walking on the road with us all along and we will say to each other, 'were not our hearts burning within us as he spoke to us through all those experiences that we felt were only secular?'

Notes

1) Jacques Maritain, *The Degrees of Knowledge, Distinguish to Unite*, ET, London, 1937, p. 132.

2) Austin Farrer, *Finite and Infinite: A Philosophical Essay*, Westminster, 1943, pp. 16ff. and 45ff.

3) Bernard Lonergan, *Insight: A Study of Human Understanding*, London, 1957, p. 678.

4) E. I. Watkin, *The Philosophy of Form*, London, 1935, p. 201.

5) L. Gilkey, *Naming the Whirlwind*, NY, Bobbs-Merrill, 1969, p. 47.

6) George Santayana, *The Realm of Matter*, NY, 1930, pp. 94 and 99.

7) L. Gilkey, *Naming the Whirlwind*, p. 315–316.

8) Peter Berger, *A Rumor of Angels*, pp. 57–68.

9) Albert Camus, *L'etranger*, Paris, 1942, ET, S. Gilbert, Middlesex, 1961.

10) Doris Lessing, *Children of Violence*, a five-volume series: *Martha Quest*, NY, 1952; *A Proper Marriage*, NY 1954; *A Ripple from the Storm*, NY, 1958; *Landlocked*, NY 1965; and *The Four-Gated City*, NY, 1969. Quotation cited here is taken from *The Four-Gated City*, pp. 61–62 and 495–496.

11) Romans 7:15–19. Jerusalem Bible translation.

12) Quoted by John Shea, *Stories of God: An Unauthorized Biography*, Chicago, 1978, p. 143.

13) Anna Blaman, quoted in *A New Catechism: The Catholic Faith for Adults* (Translation of *De Nieuwe Katechismus*, a book commissioned by the hierarchy of the Netherlands and produced by the Higher Catechetical Institute, Nijmegen, 1965, ET, London, 1969, pp. 260–261).

14) Daniel Berrigan, *Portraits of Those I Love*, NY, 1982, p. 135.

15) Doris Lessing, *The Golden Notebook*, NY, 1962, pp. 3 and 666.

16) Langdon Gilkey, *Naming the Whirlwind*, pp. 376–377.
17) G. K. Chesterton, *The Everlasting Man*, NY, 1955, pp. 112 and 114. (Wording has been slightly changed to make the language inclusive and to put the verbs into the present tense.)
18) Eric Mascall, *Existence and Analogy*, p. 85.

Part III

Recovering the ancient instinct for astonishment:
towards a concrete praxis

Chapter 7

Some contemporary spiritual exercises

THE NEED FOR A CONCRETE PRAXIS

1) *Recovering the capacity for wonder*

Mort Walker and Dik Browne are cartoonists. One of their regular cartoons 'Hi and Lois' appears in American newspapers and depicts the ups and downs of an average middle-class family. Recently one of their strips showed this family on a typical Monday morning.

In the first frame, Hi, the father of the family and an accountant by trade, is on his way to work. Driving in his car, he is saying to himself: 'Another dumb day, going to that same dumb office, to work on those same dumb numbers that I must have worked on a thousand times before!' In the second frame, his wife, Lois, is cleaning a floor and saying to herself: 'Another dumb day, cleaning this same dumb house that I must have cleaned a thousand times before!' In the next frame, we see the older children on the school bus. One is saying to the other: 'Another dumb day, going to the same dumb school, with the same dumb teachers, working at the same dumb stuff we've been working on for a thousand days already!' Finally, in the last frame, we see the youngest, Trixie, a child of about two, standing in her crib, wide awake, fresh for a new day, her arms up in the air, facing the sun, shouting in joy: '*Another day!*' In her young life, this is not just another dumb day. This is virgin time. New things will happen to her this day. She is ready to be astonished, ready for God to appear. Small wonder Jesus said that children, and those with the heart of a child, will intuit the Kingdom of God. In her attitude we see what constitutes purity of heart.

147

Conversely, in the attitude of the adults in that cartoon we see what constitutes muddied awareness, consciousness obsessed by narcissism, pragmatism, and unbridled restlessness. Theirs is the typical consciousness of everyday life and it would be them, not Trixie, who would laugh at Nietzsche's madman as he searches for God with a lantern at high noon in the market square. When we have lost our instinct for astonishment, when we meet the weekday morning with the complaining groan: 'Another dumb day!' it should come as no surprise to us that a God whom Jesus says reveals himself to the heart of a child and to the heart of a virgin will not be easily perceived. We lack the purity of heart to see God.

The previous chapters outlined three key Christian contemplative traditions, three methods for purifying awareness, for attaining purity of heart and for regaining the ancient instinct for astonishment. As presented there, however, they are more theoretical than practical, more skeleton than flesh. What needs to be outlined still is a *praxis*, a concrete set of attitudes and exercises that will help us purify our awareness and acquire the heart of a child.

2) *Contemplative exercises, not theoretical answers*

I did my doctoral thesis on the classical proofs for the existence of God. Many times, while I was writing it and since then, I have been -asked: 'Can you really prove that God exists?' 'What value do theoretical proofs for God's existence have anyway?' Most people have a healthy scepticism about any attempt rationally to prove that God exists.

Irrespective of whether such scepticism is justified, the instinct behind it has something quite important: God will not be found at the conclusion of a rational syllogism or a mathematical equation. God comes into our world, and into our minds and hearts, as Christ did when he was born in Bethlehem. God is born into life after a certain gestation process. If someone comes and says: 'Try to prove to me that God exists!', I would not spend much time trying. Instead I would tell him or her to go out and live life in a certain way, to approach reality and relationships with a certain set of attitudes. My belief is that, by doing this, they would, like Mary, the mother of Jesus, eventually give birth

148

to God in their lives. The solution to the atheism of our time is not finding better rational proofs for God's existence but a proper way of living, a proper *praxis*. If we live in a certain way, in purity of heart, God will become real.

The contemplative traditions that we outlined in the previous chapters lay out the generic direction for this *praxis*. They do not, however, lay down many of the specific disciplines we need to get there.

If our contemplative faculties are atrophied, as we have suggested, then how, concretely, do we exercise our contemplative muscles in order to restore our capacity for wonder and astonishment? What do we do to regain the heart of child? What disciplines, concretely, will help us live in such a way that we prove the existence of God to ourselves?

3) *Love is the eye*

The simplistic answer to the question just asked would be to say that we should try to meet reality as objectively as possible, without biases and preconceived notions of any kind. In this view, the more objective we are the purer we are.

Such an answer though, despite its high intention, is both simplistic and dangerous. It is simplistic because, first of all, pure objectivity is impossible. As twentieth-century science and philosophy have shown, pure objectivity is both theoretically and practically unattainable.[1] Even the strictest mathematics and science is already partly subjective. It too is a sort of poetry. The desire for pure objectivity is naive but it is also, at a point, dangerous. Pure objectivity is not only not possible, it is also not desirable. The human mind and heart are not cameras and our task in knowing is not to simply open a lens and objectively drink in reality. Knowing is a relationship and every relationship demands some active giving and some deliberate attempts to ward off blind fate (pure objectivity) so as to create meaningful destiny. Even cameras want a special angle on things and human knowing asks for far more than what one wants from a camera.

Cameras are brute, blind, heartless and that is precisely what would characterise our relationship to the world were we purely objective. Purity of heart, truly seeing the world, is not pure objectivity, the heart free of all filters. It is the heart seeing, feeling, and relating through the correct filters, the prism of love. Hugo of St Victor, a twelfth-century theologian, taught that we see correctly not by trying to remove all subjective feelings but by putting the correct feeling into the heart and mind, namely, love. He put a complete Christian epistemology into one axiom: *Love is the eye.* We see others and the world as they really are, in purity of heart, when we see them through the eyes of love. When Jesus cried over Jerusalem, he was seeing it objectively, in the deepest sense of that word.

Our task then is not to try to meet life stripped of all biases but to meet it with the correct bias, the bias of the beatitudes, the eye of love. Langdon Gilkey calls this a 'pre-ontology'.[2] Put metaphorically, a healthy pre-ontology, the bias of the beatitudes, helps us to breathe correctly. Just as we need healthy lungs physically to interrelate properly with the world, so too we need healthy symbolic lungs, a proper set of attitudes and habits, to interrelate properly contemplatively.

What are these attitudes and habits? What is the bias of the beatitudes? What constitutes a healthy set of symbolic lungs? What exercises should we do to help us maintain contemplative health so as to live in a greater purity of heart and thus come to a contuition of God?

CONCRETE ATTITUDES AND HABITS – THE PRAXIS

1) *Receptivity and gratitude*

There's a Jewish folk-tale that runs something like this. There once was a young man who aspired to great holiness. After some time at working to achieve it, he went to see his Rabbi.

'Rabbi,' he announced, 'I think I have achieved sanctity.'

'Why do you think that?' asked the Rabbi.

'Well,' replied the young man, 'I've been practising virtue and discipline for some time and I have grown quite proficient at them. From the time the sun rises until it sets, I take no food or water. All day long, I do all kinds of hard work for others and I never expect to be thanked. If I have temptations of the flesh, I roll in the snow or the thorn bushes until they go away, and then at night, before bed, I practise an ancient monastic discipline and administer lashes to my bare back. I have disciplined myself so as to be holy.'

The Rabbi was silent for a time. Then he took the young man by the arm and led him to the window and pointed to an old horse which was just being led away by its master.

'I have been observing that horse for some time,' the Rabbi said, 'and I have noticed that it doesn't get fed or watered from morning to night. All day long it has to do work for people and it never gets thanked. I often see it rolling around in the snow or bushes, as horses are prone to do, and frequently I see it get whipped. But, I ask you: is that a saint or a horse?'

To be a saint is to be motivated by gratitude, nothing more and nothing less. In the end, gratitude is the root of all virtue. It lies at the base of love and charity. Scripture always and everywhere makes this point.

Thus, for example, the original sin of Adam and Eve, the prototype of all sin, is presented to us as a failure to be properly receptive and grateful. Scripture scholars tell us that the story of the fall of our first parents, as written up in Genesis 2–3, was written many years after the ten commandments were set down and the condition that God gives to Adam and Eve, and which they violate, contains all the commandments in caption. How so?

God makes Adam and Eve and places them in the garden and showers them with goodness and life. They are given gift beyond measure and are promised that life will continue in this rich and good way, but on one condition – they are not to eat the fruit of one certain tree.

What is this condition and why does God place it on them? Essentially the condition is this: God tells Adam and Eve that they may *receive* life as gift, but they may never *take* life as if it were theirs by right. The prohibition on God's part is not some arbitrary or petty test. No. The condition that God gives them expresses an entire morality: as long as you continue to receive and respect reality as gift it will continue to give you life and goodness. Conversely, as soon as you attempt actively to seize it, or when you take it as owed, life will decrease and there will be shame, loss of harmony, pain, death, and loss of proper connection with God.

Reality is love-contoured. Hence, like love itself, it can only be received as gift. Any attempt to take it forcibly, as ours by right, amounts to rape. Adam and Eve's sin, ultimately, was one of rape, the act of taking and carrying off by force something that can only be received respectfully and gratefully as gift. It is for this reason that the story, as written in Genesis, is laden with sexual metaphor. It was not a sexual sin but what they did was in fact a form of rape.

Theologian, James Mackey comments on this.[3] He tells the true story of a man on a hunting excursion in Africa. Leaving camp one morning, the man hiked alone for several miles into the jungle where he surprised and eventually bagged several wild crane. Buckling his catch to his belt, he headed back for camp. At a point, however, he sensed he was being followed. Momentarily frightened, he stopped and looked around himself. Following him at a distance was a naked, and obviously starved, adolescent boy. Upon seeing the boy and his hunger and need, the man stopped, unbuckled his belt, and letting the cranes fall to the ground, backed off and gestured to the boy that he could take the birds. The boy ran up to the birds but, inexplicably, refused to pick them up. He, seemingly, was still asking for something. Perplexed, the man tried with both words and gesture to explain to the boy that he could take the birds. Still the boy refused to pick them up. Finally, in desperation, unable to explain what he still needed, the boy backed off from the dead birds and stood with outstretched and open hands ... waiting, waiting until the man came and placed the birds in his hands. He had, despite hunger, fear, and intense need, refused to take the birds, he waited until they were given to him. Only then did he make off with them.

This, in a manner of speaking, is the reversal of the story of the fall of Adam and Eve. Just as their story depicts the prototype of all sin, so this one demonstrates the prototype of all virtue. To be a saint is never take anything as owed, but to receive everything, gratefully, as gift.

Proper receptivity and gratitude lie at the root of purity of heart, they are the real beatitudes. Matthew 5:8 could just as easily be rendered: 'Blessed are those who are grateful, who see and appreciate everything as gift, for they shall see God.'

But gratitude like all virtues is, in the end, the result of a discipline.[4] Former generations expressed this in the slogan: *Count your blessings*. To become grateful and to remain so, it is necessary to practise the asceticism of joy. The greatest compliment that one can give to the giver of a gift is to thoroughly delight in the gift. We owe it to our creator to delight, in gratitude, in the gift of life and creation.

Thus, the first exercise we must do to restore our contemplative faculty to its full powers is to work at receiving everything – life, health, others around us, love, friendship, food, drink, sexuality, beauty – as gift. Becoming a more grateful person is the first, and the most important step, that there is in overcoming the practical atheism that besets our everyday lives. To the extent that we take life for granted we will never see the Giver behind the gift. Conversely, though, once we stop taking life for granted we will, soon enough, begin to feel it as granted to us by God.

The first proof for the existence of God is not theoretical. It is the practical reversal of the Adam and Eve story within our lives: live in deep gratitude, count blessings, and see whether God is absent from ordinary consciousness.

2) *A sense of providence and everyday mysticism*
In *The Last Temptation of Christ*, Nikos Kazantzakis places the following homily into Christ's mouth:

> Jesus' eyes flashed. Though he was in front of such a great multitude, his heart felt no fear. He parted his lips. 'Brothers', he shouted, 'open your ears, open your hearts – I ran here ... to announce the happy news for the first time. What happy news? The Kingdom of God has come'!
>
> An old man with a double hump like a camel's lifted his chaplet and cackled, 'Vague words, the words you speak, son of the carpenter, vague, groundless words. "Kingdom of heaven", "justice", "freedom", and "grab what you can boys, it's all for the taking". I've had enough! Miracles, miracles! I want you to do something here and now. Perform some miracles to make us believe in you. Otherwise, shut up!'
>
> 'Everything is a miracle, old man,' Jesus replied. 'What further miracles do you want? Look below you: even the humblest blade of grass has its guardian angel

who stands by and helps it to grow. Look above you: what a miracle is the star-filled sky! And if you close your eyes, old man, what a miracle the world within us! What a star-filled sky is our heart!'

The people listened to him, and the clay within them turned into wings. The entire time this betrothal lasted, if you lifted a stone you found God underneath, if you knocked on a door, God came out to open it for you, if you looked in the eye of your friend or your enemy, you saw God sitting in the pupil and smiling at you.[5]

Karl Rahner was once asked whether or not he believed in miracles. His reply: 'I don't believe in miracles, I *rely* on them to get me through each day.' That reply contains what we need to do in order to have a sense of God within our everyday lives. We need to rely on miracles, that is, we need to have a vital sense of divine providence within our lives. When we have that, then, as Kazantzakis' story puts it, every time we lift a stone we will find God underneath.

What is involved here? How do we develop a sense of divine providence within our lives? In the previous chapter, we analysed this philosophically and tried to show how in the tradition of philosophical theism this is done by having a proper sense of contingency within our lives. Jesus had his own expression for this. He called it *reading the signs of the times*. How do we read the signs of the times?

Some years ago, in a class I was teaching, a woman shared with us this story. She had been raised in a religious home and had been a pious and regular churchgoer. During her years at university, however, her interest and practice in religion had progressively slipped so that by the time she graduated she no longer attended church or prayed. This indifference to prayer and churchgoing continued for several years after her graduation. The story she told us focused on how all that changed.

One day, some four years after having given up all practice of prayer and church, she flew to Colorado to spend some time with a married sister and to do some skiing. She arrived on a Saturday evening and the next morning, Sunday, her sister invited her to go to Mass with her. She politely refused and went skiing instead. On her first run down the ski-slope she hit a tree and broke her leg. Sporting a huge cast, she was released from hospital the following Saturday. The next morning, her sister again invited her to come to Mass with her. This time ('there wasn't anything else to do') she accepted the invitation.

As luck would have it, it was Good Shepherd Sunday. As chance would have it, there happened to be a priest visiting from Israel. He could not see her, complete with cast, sitting in the pews and yet he began his homily this way.

'There is a custom among shepherds in Israel that existed at the time of Jesus and is still practised today that needs to be understood in order to appreciate this text. Sometimes very early on in the life of a lamb, a shepherd senses that it is going to be a congenital stray, one forever drifting away from the herd. What the shepherd does then is to take the lamb and deliberately break its leg so that he has to carry it until its leg is healed. By that time, the lamb has become so attached to the shepherd that it never strays again.'

'I may be dense!' concluded this woman, 'but given my broken leg and this chance coincidence, hearing this woke up something inside me. Fifteen years have passed since then and I have prayed and gone to church regularly ever since!'

John of the Cross once said that the language of God is the experience that God writes into our lives.[6] James Mackey, quoting George Santayana, suggests that divine providence is *a conspiracy of accidents*. What this woman experienced that Sunday was precisely the language of God, divine providence, God's finger in her life, through a conspiracy of accidents. In her response, she read the signs of the times.

Today such a concept of divine providence is not very popular. Our age tends to see it as connected with an unhealthy fatalism ('If God wants my child to live he will not let it die – we won't take the blood transfusion!'), an unhealthy fundamentalism ('God sent AIDS into the world as a punishment for our sexual promiscuity!'), or with an unhealthy theology of God ('God sends us natural and personal disasters to bring us back to true values!'). It is good that our age, for the main part, rejects such false concepts of providence. God does not start fires, or floods, or wars, or AIDS, or anything else of this nature in order to wake us up and bring us back to true values. Nature, chance, human freedom, and human sin bring these things to pass. However, to say that

155

God does not initiate or cause these things is not the same thing as saying that God does not speak through them. God is in these chance events, both in the disastrous ones and in the advantageous ones, and speaks through them. Past generations, like my parents' generation, more easily understood this.

For example, my parents were farmers. For them, as for Abraham and Sarah of old, there were no accidents – there was only providence and the finger of God. If they had good crops, God was blessing them. If they had poor crops, well, they concluded that God wanted them, for reasons that they should try to grasp and understand, to live on less for a while. They would always, in prayer and discernment, in the depths of their hearts, figure out those reasons. For them, there was no ordinary secular reality. The finger of God, divine providence, was always seen in the conspiracy of accidents that constituted ordinary life. They looked at the events of ordinary life and always tried to read the signs of the times. They stood before every event, good or bad, personal or communal, and they asked the question: 'What is God saying to us in all of this?'

They always, eventually, heard an answer. For that reason they were mystics since this is what mysticism looks like in ordinary life. This is the mysticism that Rahner highlights when he says that he relies on miracles to get him through each day. What we need to have in order to possess a sense of God's presence in everyday life, are not the kind of miracles that so drastically change ordinary reality so as to prove beyond the shadow of a doubt that there is a world of the supernatural beyond our natural world (miracle in the common sense understanding). No. What we need to have so as to move us beyond our practical atheism is a deeper sense of how God is already present and acting in the seemingly ordinary events of our lives. We need to read the signs of the times, to be able to see in the conspiracy of accidents within ordinary life, the finger of God. When we find a penny on the street, we need to have the sense that God is blessing us. Then we are mystics.

Learning to see the finger of God, divine providence, in all the events, big and small, of our daily lives is the second major spiritual exercise that is needed today. If Jesus were asked to paraphrase the beatitudes today, I suspect he might render Matthew 5:8, in the following way: 'Blessed are those who see every event of their lives against a divine horizon, who see in the conspiracy of accidents that make up their daily lives the finger and the providence of God. They will be blessed because they will not need further proofs for the existence of God!'

3) *Self-abandonment and obedience unto death*

There is a contemporary parable told about a Cretan peasant. He was a man who deeply loved his life and his work. He enjoyed tilling the soil, feeling the warm sun on his naked back as he worked in the fields, and feeling the soil under his feet. He loved the planting, the harvesting, the very smell of nature. He loved especially his wife and his children and his friends, and he enjoyed being with them, eating together, drinking wine, talking, making love, and simply being united in a shared life. And he loved Crete, his tiny country. The earth, the sky, the sea, it was his! This was his home.

One day he sensed that death was near. What frightened him, however, was not fear of the beyond for he had lived a good life. No. What he feared was leaving Crete, leaving his wife, his children, his friends, his home, and his land. Thus, as he prepared to die, he grasped in his hand a few grams of soil from his beloved Crete and told his loved ones to bury him with it.

He died, awoke, and found himself at heaven's gate, the soil still in his hand, and heaven's gate firmly barred against him. Eventually St Peter emerged through the heavy gates and addressed him: 'You've lived a good life, and we have a place for you inside, but you cannot enter unless you drop that handful of soil. You cannot enter as you are now.' The man, however, was reluctant to drop the soil and protested: 'Why? Why must I let go of this soil? Indeed, I will not! What's inside those gates I don't know. But this soil I know – it's my life, my wife, my work, my family, it's all that I know and love, it's Crete! I will not let it go!'

Silent, seemingly defeated, Peter left him and closed the large gates behind him. There seemed little point in arguing with the peasant. Several minutes later, the gates opened a second time and this time, from them, emerged a very young child. She did not try to reason with the man, nor did she try to coax him into letting go of the soil in his hand. She simply took his hand and, as she did, it opened and the soil of Crete spilled to the ground. She then led him through the gates of heaven. A shock awaited the man as he entered heaven ... there, before him, lay all of Crete.[7]

This parable illustrates what Jesus meant when he said that one of the dictates inherent in love itself is that it demands 'obedience unto death'. Love demands, by its very nature, that we continually let go of what we cling to instinctually and pragmatically so as to be open to receive that very thing in its reality and fullness. To be obedient to love, to give oneself over to its inherent dynamics, means, always, hearing the call to self-sacrifice, to self-abandonment, to let oneself be 'broken'.

All three of the contemplative traditions that we outlined previously make this point. The mystics tell us that we come to purity of heart by moving beyond ourselves; the Protestant tradition on holiness assures us that purity of heart lies in submission to the Holy; and the tradition of philosophical theism highlights the point that we are in fact always acting under obedience to some God. Thus, for all of them, purity of heart will only come when we give ourselves over to something above us.

Jesus expresses this in his own way at the end of John's gospel. After having asked Peter three times: 'Do you love me?', and being assured by Peter that he does, Jesus says to him: 'When you were younger, you girded your belt and walked wherever you wished; but when you grow old, you will stretch out your hands, and someone else will gird you, and bring you to where you would rather not go.'[8] What Jesus is telling Peter is that part of the essence of love, of any life of true self-giving, is a certain conscriptive obedience – being led, by something and Somebody outside oneself, to where one would rather not go. Dag Hammarskjold, in a famous entry in his diaries, put it this way: 'I don't know who – or what – put the question, I don't know when it was put. I don't even remember answering. But at some moment I did answer yes to someone – or something – and from that hour I was certain that existence is meaningful and that, therefore, my life, in self-surrender, had a goal.'[9]

The road beyond the practical atheism of our everyday consciousness lies in obedience and self-abandonment. If John of the Cross were your spiritual director and you went to him with the complaint that God did not seem very alive or real to you in your everyday life, he would, among other things, prescribe this exercise: 'As unpopular as this advice might be in a world that tells you, above all, to do your own thing, bend your will according to the beatitudes of Jesus. Stand before your loved ones and before your God and practise saying what Jesus said to his Father in the garden: "Not my will, but yours, be done." Then come back in a few years and tell me whether or not God still seems absent within your experience.'

4) *Revirginisation and second naivete*

If you ask a naive child: 'Do you believe in Santa Claus?' he or she will say yes. If you ask a bright child the same question, he or she will say no. However, if you ask yet an even brighter child that question, he or she will reply yes ... though now for a different reason.

This little vignette is a prescriptive counsel for the restoration of wonder within our lives. A truly contemplative consciousness, one that is truly attuned to the full depth and mystery within reality, not only *wonders-how* but it especially *wonders-at* and one wonders-at things when one has the eyes, the mind, and the heart of a child and a virgin.

Simply put, the principle here can be expressed as follows: to perceive what is most primitive and primordial in reality, we need something akin to a primitive spirit; to perceive virginal truth, we need a virginal spirit; and to consistently see the truth about the childhood of the world, we need to see the world with a certain childlike directness. To come to purity of heart we must strive constantly to live in a second naivete[10] and to, daily, revirginise.

What is involved in this process?

Revirginisation refers to a process of continually recapturing the posture of a child before reality while second naivete describes that posture as it exists in an adult who has already moved beyond the natural naivete of a child but who is not fixated in the deserts of cynicism, criticism, and false sophistication. Second naivete refers to a condition of being post-critical, post-adult, post-sophisticated. But this calls for explanation.

As children we are natural contemplatives. We spontaneously wonder at things and we see things with a certain directness. Reality, for a child, is naturally mysterious. As well, for a child, reality is all too full of the aesthetic and the supernatural. Little children, prior to the critical judgements that come with sophistication, perceive the world as laden with beauty and spirits. It is easy for children to believe in angels, ghosts, and other supernatural and mythical things; only as we mature and grow more critical, and thus approach reality with more *a priori* filters, do we grow sceptical and begin to despoil the world of its full aesthetic, mysterious, romantic, and supernatural dimensions.

But this is a necessary and a good process. A child's natural contemplative faculties are based upon, among other things, a certain naivete that would hardly be an ideal quality within an adult. As we grow to maturity, it is for our own good that our critical and practical faculties sharpen. Our naivete should disappear. However, as we hinted earlier,[11] this growth in being critical and practical is itself not an end, but simply part of a process of further development. Beyond the loss of natural naivete and natural contemplativeness lies another kind of naivete and another kind of awareness, second naivete, the awareness which returns us to the posture of a child, which sees again with the directness of a child, but has now integrated into that posture the critical and practical concerns of an adult. In natural naivete we are childish; in second naivete we are childlike.

Unfortunately, and this is especially true today in a postmodern and very sophisticated culture, the criticalness which destroys our initial naivete is taken, all too often, as an end in itself. Childishness is destroyed but there is no movement towards childlikeness. Virginity is lost but there is no movement towards revirginisation. When that happens, there sets in a certain fatigue within human perception. As Chesterton puts it, we then fall in 'the greatest of all illusions, the illusion of familiarity'.[12] This familiarity manifests itself as a tiredness of soul which Allan Bloom, the American philosopher of education, rightly calls 'eros gone lame'.[13]

Moreover, with that familiarity, almost always, there occurs a certain loss of innocence, a loss of virginity.[14] We become progressively less childlike, losing the sense of awe that is characteristic of being a child. We grow rather in experience, knowledge, and sophistication which militate against naivete. We become life-smart, and proud of it. Like Adam and Eve, after the fall, our eyes are opened. With that comes the proclivity for cynicism since life now holds few surprises, few taboos, and few sacred dimensions. In metaphorical terms, we now stand before the burning bush with our shoes on. It is not surprising that it is children, not adults, who like to go barefoot.

It is when this loss of our childish naivete and the attendant increase in criticalness, sophistication, and knowledge are not seen as part of a further development, namely, growth towards second naivete, second innocence, and second virginity, that distorted awareness and practical atheism occur in our lives. Why? Because when this happens, true agnosticism ceases and, with it, true wonder. There is an unhealthy fixation at a certain level of questioning and experiencing and there is a refusal to contemplate. Atheism and idolatry take their basis there.

Thus, if we want a more real sense of God within our lives we must move towards second naivete. We must constantly revirginise. What specifically does this entail? It entails touching the nerve of novelty, purging ourselves of the illusion of familiarity, and learning to see things as if seeing them for the first time. The answer to atheism and agnosticism is not a closed mind, but a higher agnosticism, wonder. And we move towards this higher agnosticism when we, deliberately and consciously, make the attempt to purge ourselves of all traces of cynicism, contempt, and of every attitude, however subtle and unconscious, which would identify mystery with ignorance.

This notion can perhaps best be captured by poetry. Again, let me quote G. K. Chesterton:

> When all my days are ending
> And I have no song to sing,
> I think that I shall not be too old
> To stare at everything;
> As I stared once at a nursery door
> Or a tall tree and a swing ...

> Men grow too old for love, my love,
> Men grow too old for lies;
> But I shall not grow too old to see
> Enormous night arise,

A cloud that is larger than the world
And a monster made of eyes ...

Men grow too old to woo, my love,
    Men grow too old to wed:
But I shall not grow too old to see
    Hung crazily overhead
Incredible rafters when I wake
    And I find that I am not dead ...

Strange crawling carpets of the grass,
    Wide window of the sky:
So in this perilous grace of God
    With all my sins go I:
And things grow new though I grow old,
    Though I grow old and die.[15]

What type of *praxis* leads us towards an awareness which allows us to see reality in this way? Again, let me resort to metaphor. Two metaphors are particularly helpful here.

The image of weather revirginising a geographical terrain. Imagine a geographical terrain that has been ravaged by natural disaster and despoiled by human beings. Its waters are dirty and polluted, its vegetation is dead, and its natural beauty is destroyed. However, given time and weather – sun, rains, winds, storms, frost and snow, – it, in time, will revirginise. Its waters will again grow clear and pure, its vegetation will return, and eventually its natural beauty too returns. It again becomes virgin territory. So too our hearts, our minds, our souls, and our bodies: as soon as we stop despoiling them through the illusion of familiarity, the attitude which thinks it has already understood, they too will regain, gradually, their virginity and begin again to blush in the very wonder of knowing and loving. A chastity in perceiving will return.

The image of fetal darkness. Imagine the gestation process within a womb. The process begins with a microscopic egg, a cellular speck, which is being gestated, formed, cared for, shaped by things around it, and which is nourished by a reality that is infinitely larger than itself. The process takes place in darkness, in a dark place. Eventually the child has grown sufficiently and emerges from the darkness, opens his or her eyes to the light and sees this world for the first time. The sheer overwhelmingness of what it sees so overpowers the child that it takes a long time, years of time, for the child's senses and mind to harden sufficiently so that it can begin to understand. Initially the child just looks and wonders. So too the process of being reborn, to second naivete, to new virginity. To revirginise we must, metaphorically speaking, make a recessive journey, a voyage to the sources, to the fetal darkness of the womb and be reduced again to a mere egg so that we can be gestated anew in a dark understanding that, in the words of John of the Cross, understands more by not understanding than by understanding,[16] so that we can again open our eyes and see a reality which is so wild, so startling, so agnostic, and so overpowering that we are reduced to silence, unable to name and number, able only to ponder and to wonder.

A few qualifications are called for here, however: as we said before, childlikeness should not be confused with childishness and second naivete is not to be identified with simply being naive. Second naivete is not a posture that wilfully blinds itself to hard reality and refuses to ask the tough questions. It is not a sticking of one's head in the sand or a false optimism, nor is it anti-intellectual and anti-critical. It is post-critical, post-sophisticate, post-taboo breaking. It is genuinely agnostic, fully open to wonder, believing that it knows so little and reality is so rich and multifarious that perhaps there might be a Santa Claus and an Easter Bunny after all.

And there, too, might be a God after all! Atheism is not, as is so popularly purported, the result of us, the human race, coming of age, of finally asking the hard questions with nerve and having the courage to rid ourselves of fairy tales and superstitions. Atheism, for the most part, is rooted in the opposite. It questions too little, it examines too narrowly, it is a fixation at a certain level of wonder and agnosticism. In the end, as the mystical tradition asserts, it arises out of a certain lack of chastity in perception. Jesus tells us that it is children and virgins that intuit the kingdom and see God. It is not surprising that atheism, both of the theoretical and the practical variety, has never been big on either childlikeness or virginity.

163

Thus, to exercise again our contemplative muscles so as to regain the ancient instinct for astonishment, we must work at revirginisation, at regaining the wonder, the awe, and the openness of a child. If Jesus was my spiritual director and I came to him complaining that the sense of God was habitually absent within my everyday experience, I suspect that, among other things, he would challenge me to try to get into a more vital contact with the little boy and the virgin within me.

5) *Centring prayer and the practice of contemplation*

There is a parable about our search for God that runs something like this. There was a little fish who swam up to his mother one day and asked: 'Mummy, where is this water that I hear so much about?'

The mother replied: 'You stupid little fish! It's all about you and in you. Just swim up on the beach and lie there for a while and you'll find out.'

And so there is the person who is searching for God. One day she comes up to her spiritual director and says: 'Where is this God that I hear so much about?'[17]

The parable ends there. It does not suggest what the spiritual director should say in reply. Indeed, what might the director say? God is to us like the ocean is to fish, all around us and in us. In God we live and move and have our being. If we can never get outside God how then can we keep ourselves aware of God's reality? If we are swimming in God but that reality does not seem as real to us as the reality of the heartaches and headaches of our daily lives, how can we make ourselves more aware of God?

Classical spiritual authors, not just in Christianity but within all the major world religions, suggest that one of the ways out of this dilemma is the practice of contemplative prayer. This, to cite just one example, is the basic thesis of the famous fourteenth-century English mystical treatise, *The Cloud of Unknowing*. It is also the strong motif in many of the writings emerging today from the post-Merton Trappist communities.[18] The Cistercians generally call this 'Centring Prayer', but what they advocate is in fact what older classical authors call contemplation. What is contemplation?

In classical Christian spirituality, there are two essential ways of praying: meditation and contemplation. This distinction itself is based upon a prior one: very early on in Christian spiritual writings, authors distinguished between something they called *praxis* and something they called *theoria*. *Praxis* referred to everything we can do in our attempt to reach God and others, namely, works of charity and justice, discursive prayer, and ascetical practices. *Theoria* referred to what happens within us when God and others were actually met and undergone. Hence, *praxis* refers to what is active and *theoria* to what is receptive and passive. On the basis of this, classical Christian spirituality has made a distinction between meditation and contemplation.

Thus, prayer is called meditation when we are active within it. This, for example, would be a meditation: you decide to spend a half hour in prayer. You sit down in some quiet place and pick up the Bible. You then find a text you want to meditate on and begin your prayer. You read the text slowly and try to let it speak to you. It does. You begin to feel consolation from God, challenge from God, sorrow for your sins, joy in being blessed by God. You feel yourself becoming more insightful. You pray for others. But you also experience distractions. Every so often, perhaps frequently, your mind wanders and you catch yourself thinking about other things – your heartaches and headaches. When these distractions occur, you catch yourself and bring yourself back to what you are praying about. As you are doing all of this, all this activity, all this *praxis*, you are meditating.

Contemplation, centring prayer, is quite different. Unlike meditation, which is an exercise in concentration, it is an exercise in refusing to concentrate on anything, including holy thoughts and divine inspirations. This, for example, would be contemplation: you decide to spend a half hour in prayer. You sit down in some quiet place. However, for contemplation you do not bring the Bible, nor do you bring anything to pray on or about. You begin contemplating by making a brief act of meditation. You actively focus yourself on what you are about to do, prayer, and tell God that you are here to pray, that this next half hour will be prayer. Then you calm and centre yourself, perhaps using a breathing technique and a prayer word (though these are optional). Then you begin to contemplate. What do you do? Nothing. You let your heart and mind go and you interfere in the stream of feelings and consciousness only when you catch yourself concentrating very long on anything, including holy thoughts and divine inspirations. In contemplation there is no distinction between bad distractions and holy thoughts. Everything is relative. You try to hang onto God by refusing to hang onto anything else, including thoughts and feelings about God. The whole time of prayer, save for a very brief explicit act of meditation at the beginning and again at the end, consists in this stream of consciousness and feeling. The discipline is more of not concentrating than of concentrating.

But how is this prayer? If contemplation consists simply in stream of consciousness, with a brief act of intention for prayer thrown in at the beginning and the end, by what right do we speak of this as prayer and how will that make us more aware of God? The answer to that is best understood within the analogy, the parable, of the fish and the ocean. Let us return to that story.

Imagine you are the mother fish and your child comes to you and says: 'Mummy where is this water we hear so much about?' Suppose, since this is a parable and anything is possible, you could do this. To give your child some sense of water, even though it is totally immersed within it, you could set up at the bottom of the ocean a slide projector and a television set and show your child pictures, slides, and videos of water. As ironic as it would be, these pictures, which are not water, would in fact give your child, who is living in water, some idea of what water is. Eventually, after having shown your child hours of pictures of water, you might then want to turn off all the videos and the slide projector and simply tell the child: 'Now you have some idea of what water is, you've seen pictures of it. Now I want you to simply sit in it and let it flow through you.' That image, in essence, shows what meditation and contemplation of God are.

When we pray by meditation, we are watching the slides and the videos, so to speak. All thoughts and feelings about God, even scripture itself, is not God. Good as they are, they are not the reality. At a point, they must give way to the reality – meditation must give way to contemplation – and instead of sitting and thinking and feeling *about* God we must sit *in* God. Meditation is watching the slides and the videos. It brings concepts, thoughts, and feelings about the reality. Contemplation is sitting in the reality. Normally it does not feel like prayer.

For this reason, contemplation should not be evaluated like meditation. How do you know whether or not you are praying, or have prayed? In meditation this is done during and immediately after the prayer. We are praying when we are not entertaining distractions, when our thoughts and feelings are focused on God, though even in meditation, ultimately, the effects within one's life are the real criteria which tell whether or not someone is praying. Contemplation, however, must be evaluated in a quite different manner than meditation.

Suppose you are sitting in contemplative prayer regularly, how do you know whether or not you are actually praying or wasting your time? Unlike meditation, you do not make any assessment whatever during or immediately after prayer. Instead you do contemplative prayer for a substantial period of time, several months perhaps, and then check yourself: Am I now more restful than restless; more free than compulsive; more calm than hyper; more patient than impatient; more humble than competitive; more self-forgetful than self-preoccupied; and more grateful than bitter? If there is progress in these things, then I am praying and God is more vitally within my life.

Blessed are the pure of heart, for they shall see God. If a sense of God's presence is absent within our lives, more than likely restlessness, obsessions, impatience, competitiveness, self-preoccupation, and bitterness are not. Small wonder God cannot break in! Contemplative prayer, practised regularly as a discipline, is an invaluable exercise for purifying awareness, restoring wonder, and helping us to regain the ancient instinct for astonishment.

6) *The preferential option for the poor, kissing the leper as a form of contemplation*

There is a story told about Francis of Assisi, perhaps more mythical than factual, which illustrates how touching the poor is the cure for a mediocre and dying faith:

One night prior to his conversion, Francis, then a rich and pampered young man, donned his flashiest clothes, mounted his horse, and set off for a night of drinking and carousing. God, social justice, and the poor were not on his mind. Riding down a narrow road, he found his path blocked by a leper. He was particularly repulsed by lepers, by their deformities and smell, and so he tried to steer his horse around the leper, but the path was too narrow. Frustrated, angry, but with his path clearly blocked before him, Francis eventually had no other choice but to get down off his horse and try to move the leper out of his path. When he put out his hand to take the leper's arm, as he touched the leper, something inside him snapped. Suddenly irrational, unashamed, and undeterred by the smell of rotting flesh, he kissed that leper. His life was never the same again. In that kiss, Francis found the reality of God and of love in a way that would change his life for ever.

Today many of us struggle with the same issues as did the pre-converted Francis, with a pampered life and a mediocre and dying faith. We know that our faith calls us to work for social justice and that this demand is non-negotiable. We know too, as somebody once put it with a succinctness that is praiseworthy, that strength without compassion is violence; that compassion without justice is weakness; that justice without love is Marxism; and that love without justice is baloney! What we often don't know is that the preferential option of the poor is the cure for our mediocre and dying faith. We must kiss the leper.

Simply put, if we touch the poor we touch Christ. In this way, touching the poor can be a functional substitute for prayer and, given the power of Western culture today, we often need this substitute. Let me try to explain.

Western culture today is so powerful and alluring that it often swallows us whole. Its beauty, power, and promise generally take away both our breath and our perspective. The lure of present salvation – money, sex, creativity, the good life – has, for the most part, entertained, amused, distracted, and numbed us into a state where we no longer have a perspective beyond that of our culture and its short-range soteriology.

One way out of this, of course, is through prayer. A life of prayer can cure a dying faith. The problem here, however, is that what our culture erodes in us is, precisely, our life of prayer. The hardest thing to sustain within our lives today is prayer. Everything militates against it. Given this, perhaps the only way we have of not letting ourselves be swallowed whole by our culture is to kiss the leper, to place our lot with those who have no place within the culture, namely, the poor with their many faces: the aged, the sick, the dying, the unborn, the handicapped, the unattractive, the displaced, and all those others that are not valued by the culture. To touch those who have no place within our culture is to give ourselves a perspective beyond our culture.

Daniel Berrigan, who writes eloquently on this, describes in his memoirs how much his perspective changed when he began to work full-time in a cancer ward, ministering to the terminally ill. When you walk home from work after a day of being with those who are dying, he says, your vision clears pretty well and what your culture offers to you no longer seems so overpowering and irresistible. Concrete contact with the poor is Christian contemplation. It knocks the scales off one's eyes.

'Whatsoever you do to the least of my people, that you do unto me,' Christ assures us. In the poor, God is ever-present in our world, waiting to be met. In the powerless, one can find the power of God; in the voiceless, one can hear the voice of God; in the economically poor, one can find God's treasures; in the weak, one can find God's strength; and in the unattractive, one can find God's beauty. The glory of God might indeed be humanity fully alive, but the privileged presence of God lies especially in and with the poor who, viewed through the eyes of our culture, do not appear fully alive.

Thus, like Francis, we need to get off our horses and kiss the leper. If we do, something will snap, we will see our pampered lives for what they are, and God and love will break into our lives in such a way that we will never be the same again.

THE CONTUITION OF GOD IN EVERYDAY LIFE

A hundred years ago, Nietzsche had his mythical madman smash a lantern in the marketplace at high noon and announce to Western culture that 'God is dead!' Few people took Nietzsche very seriously because, at that time, God was still very much alive in the Christian churches even if he was quite dead in everyday life. Today we, the children of Western culture, post-modern, adult children of the enlightenment, struggle with practical atheism. Our churches are slowly emptying and, more and more, the sense of God is slipping from our ordinary lives.

This problem with God, as we tried to show earlier, stems not from the fact that we are any worse than previous generations in terms of sincerity and morals, but from the fact that, for reasons whose roots go back hundreds of years in history, our consciousness today is so clouded with narcissism, pragmatism, and restlessness that we are contemplatively asleep. Metaphorically stated, we are contemplatively lame. Through too many years we have not been exercising our contemplative muscles and now they have atrophied to the point where we can no longer use them. We need some therapy. We need to do some contemplative exercises if we are to regain a vital sense of God.

The road back, however, is not that of developing a better rational and intellectual apologetic for the existence of God. Nobody is ever going to prove to anyone that God exists and that the only rational option is faith. To quote Shakespeare somewhat out of context, proofs for the existence of God only 'help to thicken other proofs that do demonstrate thinly.'[19] Nor is the road back that of miracles – apparitions, inexplicable healings, Marian appearances, and extraordinary religious experience. The God of ordinary life will be found, precisely, in the ordinary since God is a domestic not a monastic God.

The road back to a lively faith is not a question of finding the right answers, but of living in a certain way, contemplatively. The existence of God, like the air we breathe, need not be proven. It is more a question of developing good lungs to meet it correctly. God does not enter our world, or our lives, as the conclusion of a mathematical equation or a philosophical syllogism. God enters the world as the conclusion of a gestation process. We must live in such a way that we give birth to God in our lives.

This book has suggested that one kind of gestation process, the contemplative tradition within Western Christianity, is, for us today, a good road back. In a nutshell, it suggests that if we live our life in a certain way, God will be born within it and we will have no further need of any proofs or miracles – we will, instead, begin to rely on miracles to get us through our everyday lives.

What, in summary is the *praxis*?

Blessed are those who do not take life for granted, for they are within measurable distance of taking it as granted them by God.

Blessed are those who learn to see the finger of God in the conspiracy of accidents that make up their lives, they shall be rewarded with daily miracles.

Blessed are those who say yes to something higher than themselves, in that genuflection they will say the creed.

Blessed are those who take on the heart of a child and the heart of a virgin, they shall again delight in Santa and believe in God.

Blessed are those whose discipleship includes the discipline of regular prayer, they shall know that it is in God that they live and move and have their being.

Blessed are those who kiss a leper, who make the preferential option for the poor, for love and God will overwhelm them.

And blessed are those who make this a life-long quest, they will make a good beginning.

Notes

1) Pure objectivity, as contemporary physics following Einstein and Heisenberg has demonstrated, is impossible. For a popularised explanation on this, I recommend, 'Religion and the Theories of Science', in Ian Barbour's, *Religion in An Age of Science*, San Francisco, Harper and Row, 1990, pp. 95–125.

2) Langdon Gilkey, *Reaping the Whirlwind*, pp. 103–104.

3) This is Mackey's central idea in the Eucharistic theology he gives in 'Anticipatory Incompletions', in *The Christian Experience of God as Trinity*, London, SCM Press, 1983, pp. 255–258. The story itself, however, while illustrating his central idea, is not given in the book cited. It was given as an illustration as part of his lectures on the theology of the Trinity, University of San Francisco, Summer, 1979.

4) Henri Nouwen, in his recent work, *Life of the Beloved*, NY, Crossroad, 1992, lays out simply and clearly the disciplines required to become and remain grateful. See especially pp. 55–68.

5) Nikos Kazantzakis, *The Last Temptation of Christ*, NY, Simon and Schuster, 1960, pp. 189 and 301.

6) John of the Cross, *The Living Flame of Love*, Commentary on Stanza One, number 7. My expression is a paraphrase. His actual wording is: 'For God's speech is the effect he produces in the soul.' (Kavanaugh, *op. cit*, p. 582.)

7) I heard this story, in roughly this form, from John Shea. I am uncertain

171

of his source, though it seems to be a redaction and re-mythologisation of what Nikos Kazantzakis says about his own life in his autobiography, *Report to Greco*, NY, Simon and Shuster, 1960.

8) John 21:18.

9) Dag Hammarskjold, *Markings*, translated by Leif Sjorberg and W. H. Auden, London, Faber and Faber, 1964, p. 85.

10) I have taken the term, *second naivete*, from Paul Ricoeur, though my usage of the term is not, always and everywhere, the same as his.

11) See chapter 2.

12) G. K. Chesterton, *The Everlasting Man*, pp. 19 and 159.

13) Allan Bloom, *The Closing of the American Mind*, pp. 132–133.

14) Virginity here is obviously not defined in its strictly physical sense, nor is it taken to connote something primarily sexual. It refers more to a present attitude than a past sexual history and its real loss is also primarily in the area of attitude. For our purposes we define virginity as follows:

   i) It is the posture of a child before reality.

   ii) It is the attitude that allows one to live in a certain inconsummation.

   iii) It is living in such a way that there are certain areas of our person and life that are revered and sacred, and these are then shared only within a context that fully respects their sacredness. Given this sacredness, a certain number of taboos follow. Our moral freedom then restricts our radical freedom.

   Revirginisation refers to the process of recovering the attitudes and habits which allow this type of virginity to be manifest within our lives.

15) G. K. Chesterton, 'A Second Childhood', quoted by Eric Mascall, *Words and Images: A Study in Theological Discourse*, London, 1957, p. 81.

16) John of the Cross, *The Living Flame of Love*, Commentary on Stanza 3, number 48. (See Kavanaugh, *op. cit.*, p. 628.)

17) Thomas Keating, *Finding Grace at the Center*, Still River, Massachusetts, 1978, pp. 34–35.

18) I recommend especially two books by Thomas Keating, *Finding Grace at the Center* (footnote 17, above) and *Open Mind, Open Heart, The Contemplative Dimension of the Gospel*, Amity, NY, Amity House, 1986. Both lay out a good practical method of doing centring prayer.

19) William Shakespeare, *Othello*, III. iii.